AF600662

General Legislation on Indulgences

DISSERTATION

Submitted to THE FACULTY OF CANON LAW

OF THE

CATHOLIC UNIVERSITY OF AMERICA

In Partial Fulfilment of the
Requirements for the

DEGREE OF DOCTOR IN CANON LAW

BY FRANCIS EDWARD HAGEDORN

Priest of the Diocese of Kansas City

Washington, D. C.

1924

Nihil Obstat.
THOMAS J. SHAHAN, S.T.D.,
Censor Deputatus.
Washingtonensi, Die XXVII Maii, 1924.

Imprimatur.
MICHAEL J. CURLEY, D.D.,
Archiepiscopus Baltimorensis.
Washingtonensi, Die XXVII Maii, 1924.

CONTENTS

INTRODUCTION

The present treatise purposes to deal with indulgences according to their canonical aspect, that is, in so far as they form a subject about which the legislative power of the Church has been exercised. Discussion of some doctrinal phases of indulgences has been introduced into the study, but only to the extent required to furnish a foundation on which legislation might rest, an index, as it were, pointing to the reasonableness underlying certain legislative enactments. Likewise, moral and liturgical questions, while not completely eliminated, have received only that amount of attention warranted by their close relation to the canonical purpose of the book. Of necessity a somewhat more detailed treatment of the historical aspect of the subject has been given. For the study of indulgence legislation in its present estate necessarily implies a historical study. Every department of law operative at present represents a crystallization and systematization of the legal forms of the past. This is also true of the laws governing indulgences: their present status is foreshadowed in the enactments of preceding centuries. And to adequately comprehend, to correctly interpret the Canons of today, one must needs refer to the older legislation. To this end, not only has a summary chapter on the historical development of indulgences been included, but wherever expedient, historical notes have been added to the comment on the several Canons.

As indicated in the title, this treatise is confined to the consideration of those general principles and laws which are applicable to all indulgences. Particular indulgences have, indeed, received occasional notice, but only for the purpose of illustrating some point of general applicability. Both the complete enumeration of current indulgences and the detailed treatment of certain features peculiar to some of these have been committed to more comprehensive works.[1]

1 Especially noteworthy among these is the work of Beringer-Steinen "Die Ablaesse, ihr Wesen und Gebrauch," 15 edition, Paderborn, 1921-1922.

CHAPTER I.

Preliminary Notions

It seems desirable to preface these remarks on the laws governing indulgences with a summary statement of the real nature of indulgences. For although such a statement might with propriety be reserved to a dogmatic or historical treatise, nevertheless, certain canonical aspects of indulgences are so intimately connected with their nature that knowledge of the latter is much to be desired, if not absolutely necessary for the thorough understanding of the former.[1]

The Church's teaching on indulgences has ever been a target for the shafts of more or less skillful archers in the ranks of our opponents. In fact, one may doubt whether, in all the complex of Catholic dogma, there is another doctrine so much maligned as this. From Wicliffe[2] and Huss[3] at the opening of the fifteenth century, from Johann Ruchrath,[4] Wessel Gansfort,[5] and Peter of Osma[6] toward the end of the same century; from Luther[7] and Baius[8] in the sixteenth, Michael de Molinos[9] in the seventeenth, and the Jansenist-Febronian Synod of Pistoia in the eighteenth,[10] down to Lea[11] in our own age, the thread of opposition to indulgences can be traced unbroken. And—not at all a strange phenomenon—among the opponents the most vehement are often the least conversant with the subject against which they direct their attacks. Of the many who considered themselves called to malign, comparatively few were chosen to understand. Typical is the case of Luther. Not a little of Martin Luther's claim to notoriety is based on the acrimonious campaign he conducted, first against Tetzel as a preacher of indulgences, and eventually against the subject which formed the burden of Tetzel's preaching.[12] Yet Luther himself confesses, and he substantiates the confession with a confirmatory oath—"So wahr mich mein Herr Christus erloest hat"—that at the time he set out to preach against indulgences, he did not know what an indulgence was.[13] And to this ignorance, one may surmise, are to be attributed at least some of the Reformer's uncomplimentary utterances anent indulgences.

In the face of this evidence of misunderstanding so longlived and fraught with such baneful consequences, it will scarcely be amiss to introduce with some reference to the nature of indulgences a canonical dissertation on that subject.

A. ETYMOLOGY

Our word *Indulgence* is the equivalent of the Latin *Indulgentia,* which, in turn, is derived from *Indulgere.* Etymologists designate *Dulcis* as the radical element of this Latin verb.[14] Primarily, therefore, *Indulgere* conveys the idea of sweetness or suavity in one's relations with others, the manifestation of a gentle disposition, a mild and considerate mien. The substantive admits the translation tenderness, gentleness, mildness, complaisance, mercy, condescension, favor, forgiveness. Hence, according to its etymology, *Indulgentia* could be applied to the maternal affection which a mother lavishes upon a dear child, the humane treatment which a master accords his servants, the cancellation of a debtor's obligation by his creditor, a criminal's liberation at the hands of the civil authorities, God's pardon of the repentant sinner.

B. PROFANE USAGE

Indulgere and *Indulgentia* are quite frequently used by authors of both the classical and the post-classical periods. And literary usage attaches to the term a variety of related meanings. Citation of the one or other illustration culled at random from the classics will suffice. Caesar, referring to his benign treatment of the recently subjugated Haedui, says: "Aeduorum civitati Caesar praecipue indulserat."[15] In speaking of the respite which the consuls granted their worn-out soldiers, Livy says: "Indulgent consules legionum ardori."[16] The Digests or Libri Pandectarum make mention of a pardon granted to offenders as: "Abolitio reorum quae publice indulgetur."[17] The post-classical historians Julius Capitolinus[18] and Ammianus Marcellinus[19] use *Indulgentia,* the former to signify a remission of punishment imposed by judicial sentence, the latter a reduction of taxes. Later, Baronius cites a rescript of Constantine for the year 322, granting liberty to certain classes of malefactors: "Propter Crispi et Helenæ partum, omnibus indulgemus, etc."[20]

C. SCRIPTURAL USAGE

In the inspired pages of Holy Writ *Indulgere* and *Indulgentia* are to be found in eight passages. And in scriptural usage, no less than in profane, there is considerable variety in the meanings attached to these terms. First, Judith employs the noun in the sense of pardon, when in her discourse to the ancients she says: "Indulgentiam ejus (sc. Dei)—postulemus."[21] Four times the noun or the verb occurs in Isaias. His canticle of thanks contains *Indulgere* in the signification of showing favor: "Indulsisti genti, Domine, indulsisti genti."[22] Speaking in the name of the Savior, the same prophet uses *Indulgentia,* once as the release of captives,[23] and again to mean kindness.[24] Mercy is the significance of the word in a fourth passage of Isaias.[25] Two passages from the First Book of Machabees employ the verb, in the first instance to designate release from a particular tax,[26] in the second to mean the remission of a whole class of tributes.[27] Finally, St. Paul adds to his counsel of conjugal continence: "Haec autem dico secundum indulgentiam, non secundum imperium,"[28] the Rheims translators rendering: "I speak this by indulgence, not by commandment." It may be remarked that when our Savior applies to Himself the prophecy of Isaias (Is. LX, 1), He quotes, according to the Vulgate: "Misit me prædicare captivis remissionem."[29] And while the Douay translates "indulgentiam" of the Old Testament passage with "release," "deliverance" is the expression used for "remissionem" of the New Testament text.

From what has been said in the preceding sections it will be seen that the etymology of the word, its variant use among profane writers, and its employment in Holy Scripture give to *Indulgentia* a rather wide meaning, embracing almost any form of forbearance or pardon.[30]

D. ECCLESIASTICAL USAGE

The early writers in the Church applied to this word meanings as divergent as had been attributed to it in profane and sacred literature. In the course of time, however, *Indulgence* in the language of the Church came to have a narrower application, and its use was restricted to designate the forgiveness of the temporal punishments due to sin.[31] While it is undeniable that early writers use the word in this restricted sense,[32] it cannot be asserted that they used it thus to the exclusion of other meanings. In other words, *Indulgence* was not a technical expression among the early writers. It became such, however, long before the Council of Trent. For the Council speaks of "Insigne hoc indulgentiarum nomen."[33] In the estimation of the Tridentine Fathers, *Indulgence* was so well known and so definitely fixed as a technical expression that they not only designate it as an *insigne nomen,* but they deem it unnecessary to define the term. This fixing of the word in its present sense is to be attributed to the early Scholastics of the twelfth century.[34]

E. REAL DEFINITION

Until the twelfth century, Theologians contented themselves with merely accepting the fact of penitential commutations, pardons, and redemptions. Seldom did they pause to speculate concerning the precise nature of these pardons, or to formulate scientific definitions of them. Alexander of Hales may be regarded as the pioneer exponent of the theology of indulgences.[35] Yet even he does not offer a terse, formal definition. Albert the Great records two definitions known at his time.[36] Later, Duns Scotus succinctly stated his teaching on the subject in the definition: "An indulgence is the remission of the temporal punishment due to the actual sins of the repentant and left standing after sacramental absolution, a remission granted for reasonable cause by ecclesiastical prelates out of the Church's treasury, that is, the merits of Christ and the Saints."[37] Scotus' definition, embellished in form by minor additions at the hands of subsequent authors, still remains a favorite with writers on the subject.[38] To criticize these definitions or to pronounce in favor of any one of them is beyond the scope of this work, particularly since the Code provides an authoritative definition in Canon 911. Analyzing this definition of the Code into its component parts and explaining its several elements will occupy one of the chapters of the present dissertation.

NOTES ON CHAPTER I.

1 Apropos is the following criticism of Henry Charles Lea's "History of Auricular Confession and Indulgences": "In Lea's writings we see it plainly demonstrated how it does not suffice to gather with tremendous industry, material, even the most remote, but that sufficient theological learning is requisite to examine and use such material in a suitable, correct, and unobjectionable manner." Thus Baumgarten "Henry Charles Lea's Historical Writings," 40.

2 Mansi, XXVII, 1209; Denzinger-Bannwart, 622.

3 Mansi, XXVII, 1212; Denzinger-Bannwart, 676 ff.

4 Z. K. T., XXIV, 644.

5 Z. K. T., XXIV, 644.

6 Mansi, XXXII, 380; Denzinger-Bannwart, 729.

7 Grisar, "Luther," I, 263-304.

8 Denzinger-Bannwart, 1010, 1059, 1060.

9 Denzinger-Bannwart, 1263.

10 Denzinger-Bannwart, 1540-1543.

11 "History of Auricular Confession and Indulgences," Philadelphia, 1896.

12 Grisar, "Luther," I, 265-281.

13 Luther's Werke (Erlanger Ausgabe), XXVI, 50-53.

14 Freund's-Leverett's Latin Lexicon; Harper's Latin Dictionary.

15 Bellum Gallicum, I, 10.

16 Vitae, IX, xliii, 19.

17 Digesta, XLVIII, 16.

18 Vita Antonii, VI, 3.

19 Historia, XVI, 5.

20 Amort, Historia Indulgentiarum, I, 1.

21 Judith, VIII, 14.

22 Isaias, XXVI, 15.

23 Isaias, LXI, 1.

24 Isaias, LXIII, 7.

25 Isaias, LXIII, 9.

26 I Mach., X, 29.

27 I Mach., XIII, 37.

28 I Cor., VII, 6.

29 Luke, IV, 18.

30 Bellarmine, "De Indulgentiis et Jubilaeo Libri Duo," I, 1.

31 Beringer-Steinen, "Die Ablaesse," I, 1.

32 Amort, "Historia Indulgentiarum," I, i, 1.

33 Concilium Tridentinum Sess. XXV, de reform. Decretum de Indulgentiis; Beringer-Steinen, "Die Ablaesse," I, 2.

34 Paulus, "Geschichte des Ablaesses im Mittelalter," I, 212-250.

35 Otten, "Manual of the History of Dogmas," II, 373.

36 In Sent. IV, dist. 20, art. 16.

37 Quaestiones Miscellaneae, Q. IV, 4; Otten, "Manual," II, 378.

38 Bellarmine, "De Indulgentiis et Jubilaeo Libri Duo," I, i, 1; St. Alphonsus, "Theologia Moralis," VI, 531; Bouvier-Oakley, "On Indulgences," 2.

CHAPTER II.

The Early History of Indulgences

SECTION A. INDIVIDUAL INDULGENCES

Contrary to an opinion which of recent years has been gaining vogue even among Catholic scholars, one may see in the very early ages of the Church indulgences essentially identical with those granted in our own day. 'Tis true, in the first centuries there are no explicit papal, conciliar, nor episcopal concessions of indulgence. Nevertheless, in the ordinary practice of the primitive Church there are evidences of genuine indulgences so palpable that they cannot escape observation.

I. First among the early practices tantamount to indulgence is the reconciliation of penitents. Reconciliation consisted in this that the competent authority—except in extraordinary cases the Bishop—imposed hands on the penitent sinner, bringing to an end the period of his penance, and readmitting him to full communion with the faithful.[1]

To prove that in the case of reconciliation all the essential requirements of a genuine indulgence were verified, it will be necessary to take up in order: 1. the remission of temporal punishment for sins previously forgiven, this including the two points: a. that pardon of the culpa preceded the reconciliation; b. that the reconciliation removed, not the culpa, but the remnants of punishment; 2. the validity of reconciliation before God; 3. that reconciliation was extra-sacramental; 4. the question of competent authority; 5. the treasure of the Church and early indulgences.

A. Reconciliation was a remission of punishment for sins previously forgiven.

Accepted definitions of the Catholic concept of indulgences include the note that an indulgence is a remission of the temporal punishment deserved by sins that have already been pardoned. In demonstrating that this element of indulgence was realized in the ancient ceremony of reconciliation it will be necessary to indicate that an absolution from the guilt of sin preceded the reconciliation of the penitent, and, furthermore, that reconciliation effected the remission of the penalty due to sin.

a. Reconciliation was Preceded by an Absolution from Guilt.[2]

An attentive reading of the pertinent (especially of the contemporary) literature reveals that the course

An attentive reading of the pertinent, especially of the contemporary literature, reveals that the course which the penitent pursued from his defection to his acceptance of "peace" embraced the following stages.[3] First, there was confession of sin to the bishop or priest, from whom the penitent—as will be pointed out in the course of this section—forthwith received absolution from guilt (a culpa), and advice as to penance.[4] If the sins were such as demanded only private penance, the minister who heard the confession imposed the penance.[5] If, however, the exigency of the case demanded a public penance, this was regularly imposed by the Bishop.[6] During the course of penance, and on the occasion of the penitent's advance to the next of the four successive stages of penance, the Bishop repeatedly intervened to impose hands and to offer official prayers.[7] Having performed the prescribed penitential works, the sinner regularly presented himself before the Bishop on Holy Thursday for the final imposition of hands or reconciliation.[8] This was the usual procedure. In some instances the rite of reconciliation was administered by a simple priest or even a deacon.[9]

Neglecting distinctions of terminology, some writers have failed to emphasize the differences among the successive acts of the penitential rite.[10] Originally, however, there was a specific technical term for each phase. To designate the remission of guilt imparted immediately after confession (absolutio a culpa), *aphesis,* and the corresponding verb *aphienai,* were employed. *Proslambanein* designated the Bishop's first address inviting the sinner to penance. *Dechestai* and its compounds, *apodechesthai* and *prosdechesthai,* meant the actual admission to the ranks of penitents, as well as the advancement to the next of the four successive stages of penance. Finally, *apokathistanai* and *apokathistanein* signified the imparting of "peace" or reconciliation, the absolution a poena.[11] Dr. Schmitz quotes at length from standard Greek lexicographers to show that each of these four terms was used to convey the respective meanings even by profane authors.[12] The same writer is careful to point out that *aphesis* (meaning absolution from guilt) is never used in such a way as to be confused with any of the terms relating to reconciliation.[13]

To illustrate the argument, it may be well to instance the one or other passage in which the respective expressions are used. The contents leave no doubt that remission of guilt is under discussion in the following passage of the Didascalia Poenitentium given in the Apostolic Constitutions. And *aphesis* is the word used to designate that remission. "Poenitentibus autem venia concedenda est—*Aphesin didonai chre.* Nam simul ac peccator dixit ex animo sincere: Peccavi Domino! respondit Spiritus Sanctus: Et Dominus dimisit tibi peccatum *Kurios apheke soi sten hamartian.*[14] In the following, the reference to our Lord's pardon of the paralytic, whose guilt the Savior certainly removed, leaves no doubt as to the meaning of *aphesis.* "Potestatem enim habes revocandi et dimittendi confricatos cum venia—*apostellein tethrausmenous* en *aphesei.* Per te Salvator dicit paralytico in peccatis: Remittuntur—*apheontai* peccata tua." [15] Further, the Didascalia bases the forgiveness of sins on the petitions of the Lord's Prayer, wherein we unquestionably pray for the forgiveness of guilt: "Via autem pacis est servator noster Jesus Christus qui etiam nos docuit his verbis: Dimittite et dimittetur vobis—*aphete kai aphethesetai* hoc est, date peccatorum remissionem et remittentur vobis delicta—*didote aphesin hamartion kai aphethesetai* quemadmodum et per orationem docuit nos dicere ad Deum: Demitte nobis debita nostra, sicut et nos dimmittimus—*aphes hemin—hos aphiemen.*[16]

In the following citations the admission of the sinner to public penance is indicated, the second quotation presenting an instance of contrast between this admission to penance and the remission of guilt spoken of in the preceding paragraph. "Resipicentes suscipere tamquam filios *proslambanesthe.*" [17] "Leviter castigatum jamque resipiscentem susceperit *proselabeto* dismissisque peccatis *apheis auto ta plemmelemata* in regnum restituerit." [18]

The Didascalia contains at least six instances of the use of *dechestai* and its compounds, to describe the imposition of penance or the promotion to the next higher class of penitents.[19] The Council of Ancyra in its fifth, sixth, seventh, and eighth canons, uses the same expression in like meaning,[20] as also does St. Basil.[21]

Touching the final reconciliation, the Didascalia has this: "Valentem in ecclesia restitue *apokathista* et reduc ad ovile. Quod expulsum fuit revoca, hoc est, quod in poenam peccatorum suorum ejectum fuit, ne sinas foris permanere, sed assumptum et conversum redde *apokathista* gregi." [22]

From the foregoing it will be seen that—if the use of language means anything—one must admit two absolutions in the sinner's return to complete "peace," the first an absolution from guilt, the second an absolution from penalty. This conclusion is confirmed by the implication in the Apostolic Constitutions that the penitential rite had a two-fold effect: the forgiveness of sin, and the sinner's restitution to his former standing before the Church and before God. In instructing the Bishops how they might refute those who objected to a plenary reconciliation of sinners, the Constitutions say: "Nam quod Deus non solum ignoscat poenitentibus sed et eos in pristinam dignitatem restituit, abunde testatur sanctus David—dicens: Redde mihi laetitiam salutaris tui et spiritu principali confirma me."[23] The Constitutions' argument might be recast: You do not object that the Bishops remit the guilt of sin (ignoscat poenitentibus), for you are mindful that David asked for and obtained that of God (redde mihi laetitiam salutaris tui); neither ought you object if, by remitting the penalties of sin, they restore the penitents to their former place in the Church (in pristinam dignitatem restituunt), for David also begged for that and obtained it (spiritu principali confirma me).

Similar allusion to a two-fold absolution is to be found in Justin's Dialogue with Trypho,[24] in St. Cyprian,[25] and in St. Augustine.[26]

The following considerations add weight to the contention that an absolution from guilt was given before the reconciliation.

1. Under the contrary hypothesis, the sinner would have been obliged to confess the same sin twice; once, at the beginning of his penitential course, that a just penance might be imposed, and again at the time of reconciliation, in order that the minister might know from what he was absolving the penitent. That the Church, even in her primitive state, should impose such a hardship seems unlikely.[27]

2. If one assumes that no absolution from guilt was given until the end of the period of penance, then one confronts the task of adequately explaining why during twelve centuries [28] the Church not only permitted but even insisted that her children remain unabsolved and exposed to the danger of damnation for months, years, even for life [29]—and that, after they had manifested the dispositions entitling them to absolution.[30]

3. One would have to explain how one minister could absolve from sins which had not been confessed to him, but to another. For, in some instances at least, confession was made to a priest, whereas the Bishop performed the rite of reconciliation.[31] Sozomen attests the universality of this practice in the Eastern Church.[32]

4. In case an absolution from guilt had not preceded the reconciliation, deacons in the ancient Church could have absolved from guilt. For, in words that are unmistakable, St. Cyprian commits to deacons the reconciliation of penitents whom neither Bishop nor priest could reach.[33] Incidentally, this instruction of St. Cyprian is repeated by the Council of Elvira.[34] Morinus thinks that deacons had the power of giving sacramental absolution from guilt, but at the same time he admits that all the Fathers of the East and of the West hold the contrary view.[35]

5. Unless an absolution from guilt followed immediately upon confession, one faces the extraordinary

situation of the Church's occasionally ordering Viaticum to be administered to penitents in the state of mortal sin. For the third canon of the Council of Orange, held in 441, prescribes that Viaticum be given to those sinners who had accepted penance (poenitentia accepta), but had not been reconciled (sine reconciliatoria manus impositione).[36] The existence of the same practice is implied in the seventy-eighth canon of the fourth synod of Carthage.[37]

6. In case no absolution from guilt preceded reconciliation, but that reconciliation is itself an absolution from guilt, one is forced to conclude that in the ordinary course of events a simple priest had not the power to hear confessions and to absolve from sin. For the Council of Elvira states that reconciliation was the business of the Bishop and not of a priest.[38] That such was not the case, that priests did ordinarily hear confessions and absolve from guilt, though they did not reconcile penitents, is to be seen from the clear testimony of Sozomen[39] and Socrates,[40] and from the implications of Clement of Rome[41] and Origen.[42]

b. Reconciliation Actually Remitted Temporal Punishment.

Throughout the arguments advanced in the preceding paragraphs there runs the insinuation that reconciliation remitted the temporal punishments due to sin. By its very institution, this reconciliation was to relieve the penitent of the strictures imposed as canonical penalties, to restore his standing in the Church. And the restoration was not in consequence of the Church's merely ceasing to impute liability to further punishment, but was an actual pardon or absolution from punishment.[43] The complete and unreserved character of this remission will be further emphasized in a subsequent paragraph dealing with the divine ratification of ecclesiastical absolution from penance.

A more specific argument to prove that reconciliation effected the remission of temporal punishment is found in the comparison which early ecclesiastical authorities instituted between this rite and the Sacrament of Baptism. Among the Fathers Penance—and by that term the Fathers designated the penitential process as reaching its climax in reconciliation—was called a laborious Baptism,[44] a Baptism of tears,[45] a second Baptism of tears.[46] In what sense Penance is a second Baptism is set forth in the Apostolic Constitutions: "Ignitur et tu facito, O Episcope, ac quemadmodum ethnicum sacro lavacro tinctum in ecclesiam inducis post institutionem, sic et hunc per manuum impositionem, utpote poenitentia purgatum—restitue in antiqua pascha; eritque in loco baptismi manuum impositio.—Nam quod Deus non solum ignoscat poenitentibus, sed et eos in pristinam dignitatem restituat, abunde testatur sanctus David."[47] Quemadmodum tinctum, sic poenitentia purgatum," "erit in loco baptismi manuum impositio," "non solum ignoscat, sed et in pristinam dignitatem restituit," these expressions leave no doubt that in the mind of the author of the Apostolic Constitutions, so far as the effacement of the punishment of sin was concerned, reconciliation stood on a par with Baptism. And what effect had Baptism on the penalties due to sin? That Baptism removed the last remnant of such penalty was a belief held in the Church not only since the sixteenth century,[48] nor the fifteenth,[49] nor the fifth,[50] but from the very beginning.[51] If, therefore, from the earliest times Baptism was held to remit temporal punishment completely, and if the declaration of the Apostolic Constitutions "As Baptism, so the imposition of hands," was generally accepted—and the author to whom reference has just been made shows that the dictum "Erit in loco baptismi, etc.," was in reality an axiom—then one cannot escape the conclusion that the ancient Church believed that reconciliation blotted out temporal punishment.

It is true that in the passage just quoted wherein the Apostolic Constitutions compare reconciliation to Baptism, Morinus sees nothing more than a reference to the sacramental character of both rites. He adds: "Tanta vero absolutionis animae resipiscenti datae debilitas, ut ordinaria virtute sine poenitentia integram peccatorum remissionem non operatur."[52] By "integram remissionem," the author means a remission inclusive of the forgiveness of punishment; his statement, then, amounting to this, that sacramental absolution does not remove liability to punishment from that soul which has not done penance. No one denies that. The point at issue, however, is that in reconciliation there was something more involved than sacramental absolution. Morinus evidently does not hold the distinction between sacramental absolution and reconciliation, does not consider reconciliation as something added to sacramental absolution. The same criticism applies to his basing the ancient comparison between reconciliation and Baptism on the sacramental character of both, as will appear more clearly in a later paragraph wherein reconciliation is to be described as extra-sacramental.

Relative to the comparison just mentioned, Dr. Paulus makes the following remark: "Wenn auch hier Handauflegung oder Reconciliation und Taufe als bewirkende Ursachen der Suendenvergebung erscheinen, so wird doch nicht gesagt, dass beiden Institutionen auch hinsichtlich der Tilgung der Suendenstrafen dieselbe Wirksamkeit zukomme."[53] Another statement of similar import he substantiates with a reference to d'Ales.[54] Aside from Paulus' failure to distinguish between absolution from guilt and absolution from penalty in the early discipline, his dismissal of the subject with one brief sentence is too unceremonious to carry conviction, in view of the statements of the early writers.[55] Besides, if by "dieselbe Wirksamkeit" he means merely to deny that the method of Baptism's efficacy is identical with that of reconciliation, one can agree with him, for Baptism is efficacious as a Sacrament, whereas a subsequent argument will be advanced to show that reconciliation was not sacramental.

B. RECONCILIATION WAS RATIFIED BY GOD.

The rite by which penitents were released from penance was not a mere ecclesiastical ceremony, limited in its efficacy to freeing the sinner from a canonical debt contracted before the Church. Rather, it was an exercise of the power of the keys, and as such, had for its effect the loosing of the sinner from the debt of punishment he had incurred before God.[56] Reconciliation was not only valid in the eyes of the Church; it was also ratified before the divine tribunal.[57] Apropos is the verdict of Dr. Schmitz, who, after an exhaustive study of the question, comes to the conclusion that the view that reconciliation was valid only in the forum of the Church is simply untenable.[58]

That the reconciliation of the sinner was ratified by God; in other words, that the penitent, once released from penance by the Church, would not have to undergo punishment for the pardoned sin in the life to come, this is a corollary of the proposition set forth above that reconciliation remitted temporal punishment. The same reasons which argue for the reality of such forgiveness demonstrate its divine ratification. In comparing reconciliation to Baptism, in declaring "as Baptism, so is the imposition of hands," in characterizing reconciliation as a "redintegration," a "restitution to former dignity,"[59] no doubt was left that God approved and held valid the pardon granted by the Church, that He would exact no further penalty.[60]

Moreover, the official prayers offered on the occasion of the sinner's reconciliation clearly express the conviction that the sinner was being restored to complete favor, not merely in the eyes of the Church, but in the sight of God. These are the words addressed to the reconciling Bishop by the arch-priest who presented the penitents: "Redintegra in eis, Apostolice Pontifex, quidquid corruptum est, et per divinae reconciliationis gratiam fac homines proximos Deo, ut nunc jam placere se Domino in regione vivorum, devicto mortis suae gratulentur auctore." The Preface sung by the Bishop contains the following: "Clementissime Domine, hos clemens recollige et tuae ecclesiae gremio redde, ut nequaquam valeat de iis triumphare hostis; sed tibi reconciliet Filius tuus coequalis." And the absolution itself reads: "Mereantur deinceps cum justis atque sanctis in conspectu tuo adstantibus absoluti permanere."[61] Of similar import and equally explicit are the numerous reconciliation formularies collected by Morinus.[62]

C. RECONCILIATION WAS EXTRA-SACRAMENTAL.

The extra-sacramental character of reconciliation is seen chiefly in this, that the administration of the rite was sometimes confided to deacons. These were, indeed, not the ordinary ministers of reconciliation. But in the eighteenth letter of St. Cyprian [63] and in the thirty-second canon of the Council of Elvira [64] there are unmistakable proofs that in exceptional cases deacons had full power and authorization to reconcile penitents. However, it is and always has been the dogmatic teaching of the Church that the giving of sacramental absolution was reserved to Bishops and priests.[65] Hence, to regard reconciliation as a sacramental absolution is to postulate a change in the teaching of the Church, an alteration of the faith.[66]

D. COMPETENT AUTHORITY.

Reconciliation was not left to the discretion of each and every minister of the Church. On the contrary, it was reserved to the authority of the Bishop.[67] The rubrical directions in the formularies of reconciliation are all addressed to the Bishop, showing that it was under his auspices that the ceremony was performed.[68] Those Councils which introduced an abbreviation of the penitential period or a hastening of reconciliation, as the Council of Ancyra [69] and the Council of Nice,[70] are careful to specify that the shortening of penance is to be done only on the Bishop's authorization. In the exceptional cases in which priests or even deacons reconcile, it is definitely pointed out that the priest or deacon here functions only in the capacity of the Bishop's authorized delegate.[71] Finally, in protesting against the abuse of imparting reconciliation too hastily and indiscriminately on the recommendation of the martyrs, St. Cyprian bases his protest on the circumstance that those reconciliations were irregular because they were not authorized nor approved by the Bishop. And in his own forceful way, the Bishop of Carthage makes it clear that no reconciliation was valid unless supported by episcopal authority.[72]

E. THE TREASURY OF THE CHURCH.

At first sight there appears no indication that the store of Christ's merits and those of the Saints was drawn on for the remission of temporal punishment granted by reconciliation, and to that extent the claim of the reconciliatory rite to be characterized as an indulgence appears weakened. True, there is no explicit reference to such treasure. However, in many instances, the wording of the formularies of reconciliation, as given by Morinus, may be legitimately construed as insinuating recourse to such treasury.[73] Otherwise the language of many of these formularies is unintelligible. Moreover, the silence of the authorities, their failure to refer explicitly to the treasury, is no indication that they had not the treasury of Christ's merits in mind. Bellarmine's explanation of the omission of explicit reference is eminently satisfactory. He says that it is of little consequence that the Popes of those days did not say that they were granting an indulgence out of the treasury of satisfactions. For those same Popes say nothing of their applying the merits of Christ when they administer the Sacraments of Baptism and Penance. Yet everybody admits that in these Sacraments they did apply the merits of Christ.[74] A pari, therefore, they applied those merits in reconciliation.

F. OBJECTIONS.

Against the conclusion that reconciliation, being an authoritative, extra-sacramental, and divinely ratified remission of temporal punishment due to previously pardoned sins, was an indulgence, an obvious objection occurs. Briefly stated, the objection, made by Dr. Schmitz[75] and Dr. Paulus,[76] amounts to the assertion that the penalties in the early Church were blotted out by means of the penance undergone by the sinner. In other words, the remission resulted from satisfaction rendered by the penitent, and not from a cancellation contained in reconciliation. God cancelled the punishment because it had been fully atoned through penance, not because it was remitted through reconciliation. In support of this view, Dr. Schmitz adduces a number of pointed passages from the Epistles of St. Cyprian wherein the African Bishop's reprimanding certain contemporaries for having reconciled penitents too soon is made to signify that reconciliation was nothing more than an official approval of a perfectly performed and wholly effectual penance.[77]

This objection would reduce reconciliation to a mere ceremonial, void of real efficacy. And so to reduce it seems to do violence to the mind of early writers and councils. Had reconciliation been a rite productive of no effect, one should not see, as may be seen, council after council insisting upon its being conferred, and legislating in matters of its most minute details. Dr. Schmitz would save the situation by the following device: Reconciliation did have some efficacy. In imposing penance, the confessor had no assurance that the amount he imposed was adequate to meet the debt due to God. But, that penance having been discharged and reconciliation having been imparted, the Church held that the sinner, so far as temporal punishment was concerned, stood on a par with the newly baptized, free from all debt. Now, the part of reconciliation, says Dr. Schmitz, consisted in compensating for the possible difference between the confessor's assessment of penance and the amount of satisfaction demanded by God.[78] Assuming Dr. Schmitz's analysis to be correct, even then there was an indulgence granted. For the Church declared cancelled—and her declaration, be it remembered, was ratified before God—that part of the liability to punishment by which the demands of God exceeded the assessment made by the confessor: an authoritative, extra-sacramental remission of punishment due to pardoned sins.

The contention of Dr. Paulus is that the sinner's penitential works satisfied the divine justice, so far as it was satisfied here below.[79] However, the learned author himself maintains that those penitential works were imposed without any assurance of their adequacy.[80] The Church did not, and could not, assert that, for example, at the end of ten years' penance the sin of adultery was fully expiated in God's sight.[81] Yet, as has been seen, the Church did declare that at the end of that period of penance, and after reconciliation had been imparted, God held the sinner accountable for no more. Therefore the Church took upon herself to authoritatively cancel or remit the difference—and in some instances it may have been a considerable difference—between the satisfaction rendered by the sinner and the atonement demanded by God. And that, in final analysis, is precisely what the Church does today when she grants an indulgence. In the power of binding and loosing conferred by Christ, the Church had full warrant for making the cancellation. The exercise of that power, endued with the qualities described in the preceding paragraphs, constituted the granting of an indulgence as real as the formal indulgences of the twentieth century.

The conclusion is, then, that wherever and as long as solemn reconciliation was imparted in the Church, there the Church granted plenary indulgences to the reconciled individuals.[82]

II. Intercession of the Martyrs.

During the age of persecution, the martyrs exercised an influence on penitential discipline. Christians who, having yielded to the blandishments or the threats of the persecutors and having sacrificed to idols, later repented and submitted to penance, were wont to appeal to the good offices of the martyrs for a mitigation of the penitential severity. To effect a relaxation of the rigor of penance, the martys took no authoritative steps. Instead, they furnished their suppliants with a "libellus pacis," in which they entreated mercy for the sinner in view of their own sufferings for the faith. These libelli were then presented to the Bishop, who usually took cognizance of them, and forthwith admitted the bearer to reconciliation.[83]

Before examining the relation to indulgences which these relaxations of penance possess, it will be of interest to note the attitude of two early authorities toward this unique intervention of the martyrs. Tertullian is frequently thought to have repudiated the value of the martyrs' intercession as remissive of penance. And his words: "Who will permit a man to grant those things the giving of which is reserved to God? Let the martyr be content with having paid his own debts,"[84] leave no uncertainty as to his mind in the matter. It should be remembered, however, that those words were penned after Tertullian's defection, and, therefore, while they may represent the view of Tertullian the Montanist, they do not represent Tertullian the Catholic. For before becoming involved in Montanism, he had written to the martyrs: "Your peace is war to him (the devil). Some, not having that peace in the Church, are wont to implore it of the martyrs in prison. And therefore ought you have that peace in yourselves, and nurture it and guard it, so that you may be able to grant it to others."[85] Moreover, whatever may have been Tertullian's opinion before or after his fall, the first quotation above, occurring as it does in the context of a criticism of contemporary Catholic practice,[86] proves that at the time it was written the orthodox authorities gave full value to the intercession of the martyrs.

The issuing of "libelli pacis" was especially prevalent at Carthage. Hence it is to the Bishop of Carthage that one may look for an expression of opinion on the subject. St. Cyprian expressed his estimate of the value of the intercession of the martyrs as follows: "Those who have received letters of peace from the martyrs can be aided before God by reason of the prestige of the martyrs."[87] "I think we should come to the relief of our brethren, so that those who have obtained letters of peace from the martyrs may be aided before God by reason of their prestige."[88]

But at least one writer objects that St. Cyprian taught that the intercession of the martyrs on behalf of penitents would become effective only on the day of general judgment.[89] Of what precise advantage such intercessions would prove on the last day, long after the penitents should have expiated their sins by personal atonement, the author does not attempt to make clear. In proof of St. Cyprian's supposed attitude toward the immediate inefficacy of the martrys' letters, Dr. Paulus quoted from "De Lapsis": "We believe, indeed, that the merits of the martyrs and the works of the just have great influence with the Judge, but not until the day of judgment, when, after the destruction of this world, the people stand before the Tribunal of Christ."[90] The quotation is not apropos. The context is not concerned with the merits of the martyrs as applied to penitents by means of the letters of peace, but is concerned with those merits of the martyrs as being meritorious for the martyrs themselves. In this light, St. Cyprian's remark amounts to no more than the commonplace observation that the merits of the martyrs and the works of the just are rewarded by God, not in this life, but in the life to come.

That the Bishop of Carthage regarded the "libelli pacis" quite differently is apparent from the same work: "If the martyrs ask that a thing be done, if that thing be just, if it be licit, then it must be done by the priest of God."[91] St. Cyprian certainly held that in deference to the intervention of the martyrs, the sinner's period of penance was to be cut short, and reconciliation imparted by the competent authority. In accordance with this view, he was quick to suppress incipient abuses of the practice, to regulate the issue of the letters of peace. He raised his voice against the misdirected zeal of certain martyrs who had issued letters without previously examining the deserts of their suppliants, even before confession had been made and penance imposed. He declared against the abuse of issuing letters which could be communicated to the relatives and friends of the original recipient. By insisting that care and discrimination be shown in the issue of the letters, St. Cyprian gave proof of his high regard for the letters that had been rightly issued and evinced his intention of keeping up the high standard of these letters against those who would have reduced them to the commonplace.[92] Finally, there is record of at least one such letter which Cyprian himself, whilst languishing in prison in 250, issued in favor of Candida and Numeria, the execution of which he committed to Celerinus.[93]

This abbreviation of penance in consequence of the intercession of the martyrs was a genuine indulgence granted by authority of the Church. It was a remission of temporal punishments due to previously pardoned sins,[94] punishments which should otherwise have been expiated by enduring the canonical penance. It was valid before God, as is indicated in the typical citations just adduced from Tertullian and St. Cyprian. It was extra-sacramental according to the tenor of the exposition made in a preceding paragraph. That the treasure of the Church was drawn on in the granting of these remissions is apparent from the very nature of them. For it was in view of the supererogatory character of the martyrs' satisfactions that their letters had any weight whatever. Moreover, the objection preferred by Tertullian: "Let the martyr be content with having paid his own debts,"[95] clearly indicates that the common teaching against which Tertullian protested held that the martyrs' intercessions were applicable to penitents because these martyrs had stored away a fund of satisfaction in excess of their personal needs.[96]

III. Mitigation of Penance by Councils.

A word may be said concerning the mitigation of penitential discipline brought about by the action of certain councils in the early centuries. To some writers[97] such conciliar legislation represents the granting of genuine indulgences. There are others who deny that these mitigations were indulgences in the accepted sense of the word.[98]

As the first illustration of the reduction of penitential rigor, the enactments of the Council of Ancyra may be cited. Deacons, says the Council, must refrain from exercising their ministry while doing penance. But the Bishop may regard the deacons' labor and humility and reduce this penalty. "The regulation of these matters is left to the discretion of the Bishops."[99] The fifth canon of the same Council enacts that those who have sacrificed to idols only with reluctance should undergo but three years' penance. At the same time the Bishops are to examine the previous manner of life of these penitents and either reduce or add to this three years' penance, according to the dictates of priestly prudence.[100] Likewise, the Council of Nice, after prescribing a penance of three years for those who had begun penance and then relapsed, adds that the Bishop may lighten this burden in the case of those who by tears, submission, modesty, and zeal show themselves worthy of the mitigation, but that those who show no such dispositions should by all means be kept under discipline for the full period.[101] The twenty-first canon of Ancyra relates that a former law imposed life-long penance on those guilty of fornication and feticide;[102] but the Council of Ancyra reduces this to a period of ten years.[103] Likewise, the twenty-third canon of Ancyra reduces the former penance of seven years for involuntary homicide to five years.[104]

These and similar conciliar enactments of later times do not, in the opinion of Dr. Paulus [105] constitute the concession of indulgences. And that opinion seems entirely acceptable. The reason is this: In the second canon of Ancyra, the first quoted above, Bishops are empowered to relax, at their discretion, the rigor of penance imposed on recalcitrant deacons. It is to be noted, however, that the relaxation is accorded, not in consequence of any intercession, not by application of the merits of any third party, but solely in view of the penitents' extraordinary zeal in the performance of their penance: "Conscii sint episcopi laboris eorum, humilitatis et mansuetudinis." In reality, the Bishop's action does not import a relaxation at all, but merely a taking cognizance of the increased fervor of the penitent. The penitent pays the full penalty, compensating by his intensity for the abbreviation in time.[106] And as St. Leo the Great [107] and St. Basil [108] remark, it is intensity no less than duration that God takes into account in weighing the value of penance. But a relaxation granted in deference to the penitent's own work of zeal is not to be accounted an indulgence.[109] This direction which the Council of Ancyra gives to Bishops is comparable to the sound advice given to confessors in our day: "A less severe penance than would otherwise have been imposed may be given if the penitent is extraordinarily contrite."[110] If the modern confessor, following this advice, does not grant an indulgence, neither did those Bishops who carried into effect the injunction of the Council of Ancyra.

What has just been said of the second canon of Ancyra applies with equal force to the fifth canon of Ancyra and to the twelfth canon of Nice, both cited above. For neither of these contains more than the instruction that Bishops take regard of "the manner of life, the tears, the submission, and the good works of the respective penitents," and exercise compassion accordingly.

Not very different is the import of the twenty-first and the twenty-third canons of Ancyra. These canons simply represent the introduction of a new penitential law, milder than that which had hitherto prevailed; a thing essentially different from the concession of an indulgence, which implies the jurisdictional remission of a penance already imposed.[111] These canons do not, as the cursory reader may at first surmise, mark the beginning of the era of indulgences, nor even a stage in that era's expansion. They rather indicate a step in the process by which the penance of primitive times, of long duration and great rigor, was mitigated to its present mildness. These first evidences of mitigation contained in the canons of Ancyra are no more a concession of indulgences than is the approved modern custom which warrants the imposition of merely a few decades of the Rosary on the modern penitent.

IV. Redemption of Penance.

The seventh century witnessed the introduction of a new factor into penitential discipline. This was the so-called redemption of penance. Redemption consisted in this, that the penitent commuted or substituted alms to the poor or the recitation of prayers for the corporal chastisements, such as fasting, that had been imposed in penance.[112]

A distinction has to be made between the authorized redemptions and those made on private initiative. To the latter class belong the earlier instances of the practice. The home of these redemptions was the Church of Ireland and England, where the so-called Canones Hibernenses and various Penitentiales contained systematized formularies by which long periods of penance might be replaced by redemptions payable in a few days. The migration of the Irish monks transferred the practice of redeeming penances to the continent, where it spread apace.[113]

It was characteristic of this kind of redemption that in it the works substituted for the canonical penance were substituted at the penitent's free choice, under the impression that the work chosen had an objective worth equal to the canonical penance. An authoritative foundation or approval of such substitutions is hard to find. They are ascribed, now to Venerable Bede, now to Egbert, now to Theodore of Canterbury, without any proof that these men are responsible even for the penitential books describing the redemptions.[114]

The ecclesiastical authorities were not favorable to these private redemptions from the very outset. Dr. Schmitz records that as early as 560 a Synod of Landave forbade a local redemption of penance.[115] In 747 the Synod of Cloveshave declared redemptions "a new invention, a dangerous custom," and said that "alms may not be offered in order to diminish or alter the satisfaction by fasting and other expiatory works imposed by the priest in accordance with Canon Law."[116] In 813 the Synod of Chalons declared in reference to private redemptions: "We repudiate and desire to completely eliminate those lists called penitentials, the errors of which are certain, the authors uncertain."[117] A Synod of Paris in 829 demanded that the penitentials should be burned wherever found.[118] Finally, the Synod of Mainz in 848 declared that these penitentials savoring of laxism should be replaced by others in which the manner and duration of penances should accord with the ancient canons.[119] This prescription of the Synod of Mainz, Dr. Schmitz proves, was carried into effect, the new penitentials containing no reference to redemptions.[120]

It is impossible to regard as indulgences these redemptions introduced at the will of the penitent. Of undetermined origin, always frowned upon by the authorities, and eventually suppressed, they lack the first requisite of a true indulgence: concession, or at least approval, by competent authority. Dr. Schmitz summarizes the case against them, saying: "The rejection of the penitential books which contained redemptions is an incontrovertible argument against the assumption that the concession of indulgences was associated with redemptions."[121]

Distinct from private redemptions were those instituted or acknowledged by the authorities. The first instance of such authorization occurs in the Synod of Tribur in 895.[122] This Synod declared that those doing seven years' penance for murder might, during the last six years, substitute for the fast prescribed for Wednesdays, Thursdays, and Saturdays, an alms sufficient to feed three paupers.[123] Subsequent approved redemptions are to be found in the Synods of Rheims in 923 and of Winchester in 1070.[124] St. Peter Damian, acting in the capacity of papal legate, granted the Archbishop of Milan the option of redeeming a hundred years' penance imposed for simony.[125]

Were these authorized redemptions indulgences? In the opinion of Morinus,[126] Dr. Paulus,[127] and Dr. Schmitz,[128] they were not. And the reasons alleged by these authors carry conviction. Redemptions were not remissions in any adequate sense of the word, but were merely commutations of prescribed penance into some other form of satisfaction, whose objective value equalled the values of the original penance. "The characteristic of these redemptions is the basic idea that the work substituted had an objective value equal to the canonical penance."[129] By redemption, therefore, the penitent satisfied the canonical claims as well as the demands of divine justice, not by drawing from the treasury of others' satisfactions, but by personally paying his debt in equivalent works. But the idea of indulgence precludes a remission gained through one's own satisfaction.[130] The conclusion is that redemptions, whether privately initiated or legitimately authorized, were not indulgences.

V. Roman Pilgrimages.

Contemporaneous with the era of redemptions was the practice of making pilgrimages to Rome to obtain a mitigation of penance. Rome, glorious throughout Christendom by reason of its possessing the tombs of the Blessed Apostles, as being the See of the Vicar of Christ, was naturally a favored place of pilgrimage. As is recorded in the life of the Blessed Ulrich of Zell, people were wont to journey to Rome and at the tombs of SS. Peter and Paul pray for the remission of their sins.[131] At first, however, there was no hint that a true indulgence could be gained by these pilgrimages. And if such expressions as "pro peccatis suis redimendis," "pro redemptione peccatorum meorum," "ut ibi peccatorum nostrorum veniam impetrare mereamur," indicate the motive which drew pilgrims Romeward, those expressions do not argue that indulgences were granted there, but rather they attest the belief that the good work of a pious pilgrimage, devout personal prayer, and the intercession of the Apostles were means of drawing down the divine mercy on the pilgrims and of obtaining pardon for transgressions.[132]

Roman pilgrimages made with a view of gaining a remission of penance had their beginning in the eighth century.[133] The practice seems to have originated in the circumstance that in the case of certain crimes, among them being unpremeditated homicide and certain species of unchastity, difficulties arose as to the imposition of penance. And for the solution of these difficulties, the sinner was frequently ordered to Rome, where the Supreme Pontiff attended to the case.[134] The next step occurred when the perpetrators of particularly heinous crimes were sent to Rome in order that the Pope might impose condign penance or determine that a comparatively light penance sufficed. Mention of this is made by Dr. Schmitz, quoting from a ninth century penitential: "If anyone kills a man in Orders, or his nearest blood relative—let him go to the Pope at Rome and afterwards do as the Pope shall prescribe."[135] It was customary for the Pope to send the penitent back to the Bishop with a rescript designating the penance which the latter was to impose.[136]

In all such instances, the Pope was wont to do the one or the other of two things. Either he would take cognizance of certain dispositions of the penitent and impose a milder penance than was usual. As an instance of this, Morinus quotes a letter of Pope Nicholas I to Hincmar of Rheims, in the interest of a homicide: "The period of his penance should have been extended until death, but because of his devout faith and because he hastened to enlist the suffrages of the Apostles, we have dealt more kindly with him."[137] This was not an indulgence, properly considered, but merely an imposition of lighter penance in view of the penitent's dispositions: his demonstration of lively faith and his pilgrimage to the holy tombs. Or, on the other hand, the Pontiff's rescript might impose the usual penance, but stipulate that the Bishop was at liberty to remit a part of it. An illustration is found in the letter of Pope Alexander II in the case of an infanticide: "If any Bishop desires to mitigate this penance somewhat, by apostolic authority We permit him to do so."[138] Here is a genuine indulgence, a remission of penance granted by the Bishop as delegate of the Holy See.[139] More than this, the Popes sometimes personally granted the pilgrim a remission of penance imposed by his Bishop. As early as 877 Pope John VIII sent back a pilgrim with the injunction that his penance be lightened.[140] Ten years later, at the request of the Bishop of Le Mans, Pope Stephen V granted a remission to a woman guilty of infanticide.[141] Alexander II also granted remissions of two years and of one year, respectively, to two penitents from the dioceses of Coutances and Padua.[142]

It is probable that Boniface VIII had in mind such instances of indulgenced pilgrimage when, in publishing the first Jubilee Bull in 1300, he wrote: "A reliable tradition of the ancients has it, that generous remissions and indulgences of sins were granted to those who approached the honored basilica of the Prince of Apostles at Rome."[143] Undoubtedly it was to this and to the other examples of genuine indulgence mentioned in the preceding paragraphs that the Council of Trent made reference when it declared: "Since the power of granting indulgences has been in use in the Church, even from the most ancient times, etc."[144]

SECTION B. GENERAL INDULGENCES.

The indulgences thus far referred to contain a common note, a characteristic which distinguishes them from the modern forms. Indulgences granted in early times were individual concessions, favors bestowed in single instances on particular persons. On the contrary, the modern indulgence, as a rule, is a general grant, the fruits of which all, or at least very extensive classes may enjoy. The transition from the former to the latter species took place in the course of the eleventh century,[145] although various factors, not the least of which were the redemptions of penances, had long since been preparing the way.[146]

I. Indulgences for Alms and Visiting Churches.

The earliest of these general indulgences were those granted for visiting churches and for almsgiving. The former may be regarded as the complement of the particular remissions associated with the Roman pilgrimage; the latter are the corollary of penitential redemptions.

Early general indulgences for visiting churches and giving alms were granted by both Bishops and Popes, the former preceding the latter by a few years. As the first instance of a general episcopal indulgence, reference is sometimes made to a concession in 1019 by Archbishop Pontius of Arles in favor of the Abbey of Montmajor.[147] However, evidence is at hand to prove that this reputed concession was not only of later date, but that it was an invention, pure and simple, of the inmates of Montmajor, who also invented a similar concession in favor of the affiliated Cloister of Correns and claimed the concession was contained in a Bull of Sergius IV, presumably issued in 1010.[148]

The first adequately attested concession of a general episcopal indulgence appears in 1035. It was concurred in by four Bishops: Guifred of Narbonne, Guifred of Carcassone, Guislabert of Barcelona, and Ermengaud of Urgel. A remission of one day's penance each week was granted to those who visited and contributed to the Abbey Church of San Pedro de Portuno.[149] At the same time a similar indulgence was granted to all who contributed one "denare" to the support of the Brotherhood founded at San Pedro.[150]

Not so fully proved is a remission of one half of all penance, supposed to have been granted by a number of Bishops in favor of benefactors of the Church of St. Fides in Conques, between 1044 and 1052.[151].

Benefactors of the Church of Notre Dame d'Arles were granted a year's indulgence by Bishop Guifred of Narbonne in 1046.[152]

Another indulgence that is unquestionable was granted in 1050 by Bishop Deodatus of Toulon to the visitors and benefactors of the Church of Pierrefeu. As in the case of the San Pedro indulgence, a remission of one day's penance was granted for every day of the week during one year. However, the seasons of Advent and Lent were excepted.[153]

It will be seen that authentic general indulgences granted by the Bishops in the eleventh century were few. The close of the eleventh century and the course of the twelfth saw the practice spread from the place of its origin—Northern Spain and Southern France—

to other parts of the continent, so that during the twelfth century indulgences of Bishops were quite common,[154] in fact, excessive, as appears from the restrictions which the Fourth Lateran Council in 1215 placed on the episcopal granting of indulgences.[155]

General papal indulgences came somewhat later. Until the second half of the eleventh century there is not a single papal concession that can claim to be genuine.[156] Reference is sometimes made to a grant of Gregory the Great in favor of St. Peter's Church in Mantua, by the terms of which visitors of the above church would "doubtless receive the same pardon and apostolic benediction as could be received by visiting the tombs of the Apostles."[157] Aside from the fact that this letter is spurious,[158] its tenor does not necessarily imply the granting of an indulgence. The "veniam" it mentions may well refer to a pardon of guilt, to which the pious visit to the church and the alms given on the occasion would dispose. Likewise spurious is the privilege which Pope Agatho is supposed to have granted to St. Peter's Church in Medeshampstead.[159] Other indulgences falsely attributed to Popes are those of Benedict VIII to the Benedictine Abbey of Neuburg in 1020,[160] and to the Monastery of St. Benignus in 1024;[161] that of John XIX to the Cathedral of Aquileia in 1031;[162] of Benedict IX on the occasion of the dedication of the Abbey Church of St. Victor in Marseilles in 1040;[163] of Leo IX in favor of the Abbey of Subiaco in 1051.[164]

In the latter part of the eleventh century genuine papal concessions of general indulgences began to appear.[165] In 1060 Pope Nicholas II dedicated the altar of the Abbey Church of Farfa. According to the testimony of a witness of the ceremony, the Pope granted an indulgence of three years to those present, which indulgence could also be gained on the anniversary by those who contributed to the church according to their means, or at least visited it.[166] Dr. Paulus admits that this concession is so well attested that it cannot be dismissed as spurious.[167] In 1070 Alexander II granted an eight days' indulgence to all who visited the church he dedicated at Lucca.[168] In 1091 and again in 1096 Urban II granted general indulgences of the fourth and seventh part of imposed penances. The former was in favor of the benefactors of the Pavilly Abbey,[169] the latter for the benefactors of St. Nicholas' Abbey Church in Angers.[170]

As was the case with episcopal indulgences, so, too, general papal indulgences, comparatively rare before the twelfth century and very moderate at first, soon became quite numerous and much more generous.

II. Crusade Indulgences.

As an example of the increased frequency and liberality of papal indulgences, one may cite the concessions made on the occasion of Crusades. Some difference of opinion exists as to the granting of the first Crusade indulgence. To John VIII is often ascribed the granting of the first such indulgence, and incidentally of the first indulgence in behalf of the dead.[171] As a matter of fact, that Pope merely granted an "absolution" to those who had fallen in the war against the pagan. That such an "absolution of the dead" was no more a concession of indulgence than is the modern "absolutio ad tombam," Dr. Paulus proves beyond the possibility of a doubt.[172]

The first Crusade indulgence was granted by Alexander II in 1063: a plenary indulgence to all participants in the war against the Moors in Spain.[173] It is strange that the issue of the first Crusade indulgence is almost unanimously attributed to Urban II, and the previous concession of Alexander is quite generally overlooked. Perhaps the attribution to Urban is to be explained by the circumstance that the latter's grant was in connection with the first Crusade to the Holy Land, and the popular notion tends to restrict the term Crusade to expeditions undertaken for the rescue of the holy places in Palestine. Urban's indulgence was published at the Synod of Clermont in 1096.[174] From that year until 1537, Amort enumerates no less than eighty-five concessions and ratifications of plenary indulgences to be gained by those who bore arms against the Turks, the Albigenses, the Hussites, the Moors, the Saracens, and various other enemies of the Faith.[175]

III. The Jubilee Indulgence.

Says a recent writer: "There has always been a certain mystery surrounding the origin of the Anno Santo or great Jubilee, first proclaimed, as far as our records have hitherto enabled us to ascertain, by Pope Boniface VIII in the year 1300.[176] The author then refers to the introduction of Boniface's Jubilee Bull, the "Antiquorum habet fida relatio,"[177] and to a recently discovered Latin poem found in a thirteenth century Florentine manuscript.[178]

From these two sources Father Thurston draws support for the tradition that the institution of the Jubilee antedates Boniface VIII by more than a century. However, the "Antiquorum relatio" of Boniface's Bull is adequately explained—as has been noted above —[179] by restricting its reference to the indulgences which Popes were wont to grant in individual instances to Roman pilgrims. The tradition of which Boniface speaks scarcely admits of application to so widespread and general a remission as a Jubilee implies. As for the poem, it used the word Jubilee, indeed: "Anni favor jubilaei Poenarum laxat debitum." But the entire context proves that the poet had in mind not a special form of indulgence, but the usual indulgence granted to crusaders against the Albigenses, probably the one published by Innocent III in 1208.[180] If the poet chose to call this Crusade indulgence a Jubilee, his choice of a name does not alter the nature of the indulgence, does not constitute a real Jubilee indulgence. In fact, an indulgence of any kind contains the elements of remission connoted by the Jubilee of Deuteronomy, and for this reason any indulgence might be called a Jubilee in a very wide sense. It was thus that Isidore of Seville could say: "Jubilaeus interpretatur remissionis munus."[181] Therefore, in the absence of evidence to the contrary, one may continue abscribing the institution of the Jubilee to Boniface VIII in 1300.[182]

Originally, the year of Jubilee was to be observed at the opening of each century, but already in 1343 Clement VI abbreviated the interval to fifty years,[183] so that the second Jubilee indulgence was to be gained in 1350. In 1475 Pope Sixtus IV fixed the period of recurrence of the Jubilee at twenty-five years, and this interval has been observed since that time.[184]

To sum up: History bears witness that the power of granting indulgences has been exercised by the Church from the earliest times. For a long period indulgences took the form of favors bestowed on individuals in particular cases, the solemn reconciliation of penitents and the abbreviation of public penance in deference to the martyrs' intercession being typical illustrations of this form of indulgence. The eleventh century saw the rise of the general indulgence, the first instances being those granted for visiting churches and giving alms. With the promulgation of Crusade and Jubilee indulgences, the general indulgence became widespread, and the development of indulgences was essentially complete. Thenceforth, it remains for the historian to examine the rapid multiplication of indulgences, for the dogmatist to discuss and criticise the great mass of theological literature which, beginning with the early Scholastics, grew up around the doctrine of indulgences.

NOTES ON CHAPTER II.

1 Kirchenlexicon, art. "Bussdisciplin," II, 1569.
2 Pesch, "Institutiones Dogmaticae," VIII, 265, 496.
3 Tanquerey, "De Poenitentia," 694-695; Der Katholik, 1885, 351.
4 Der Katholik, 1885, 357, quoting Sozomen, VII, 16.
5 Der Katholik, 1885, 358. Cf. Rauschen, "Eucharist and Penance," 196.
6 Der Katholik, 1885, 358, quoting the Ordo and Pontificale of the Synod of Agde.
7 Pesch, "Instit. Theol.," VII, 81.
8 Tanquerey, "De Poenit," 694-695; St. Cyprian, Ep. XV, in Kirch, "Enchiridion Fontium Historiae Ecclesiasticae Antiquae," 267.
9 St. Cyprian, Ep. XVIII, in Kirch, "Enchiridion," 271.
10 Morinus, "De Poenitentiae Sacramento," III, v.
11 Pesch, "Institutiones Dogmaticae," VII, 496; Der Katholik, 1885, 351 ff.
12 Der Katholik, 1885, 356, quoting Henricus Stephanus, "Thesaurus Graecae Linguae," VIII.
13 Der Katholik, 1885, 252.
14 MPG. I, 630.
15 MPG. I, 634-642.
16 MPG. I, 634, 651.
17 MPG. I, 623.
18 MPG. I, 650.
19 MPG. I, 618, 623, 634, 642.
20 Mansi, II, 519.
21 Ad Amphilochium, Ep. III, MPG. XXXII, 803.
22 Der Katholik, 1885, 355.
23 MPG. I, 602, 598.
24 Dial. cum Tryph., cxli, MPG. VI, 798.
25 MPL. IV, 252.
26 Ep. ccxxviii, 8, MPL. XXXIII, 1016.
27 Pesch, "Institutiones Dogmaticae," 267.
28 Der Katholik, 1885, 349: "Dagegen ist eine sich gleichbleidende Uebung bis zum 13 Jahrhundert darin zu beobachten, dass das Mass der Bussdauer nach den Canones der Kirche bestimmt wurde—und der Busser am Schlusse der Busszeit die feierliche Reconciliation erheilt."
29 Cf. penitential lists in Morinus, "De Poenitentiae Sacramento," Appendix, 7; also the Canons of the Council of Ancyra, Mansi, II, 519.
30 Pesch, "Institutiones Dogmaticae," VII, 267.
31 Pesch, "Institutiones Dogmaticae," VII, 266.
32 Der Katholik, 1885, 357; Eusebius, "Hist. Eccl.," VII, xvi, in MPG. LXVII, 1459.
33 Ep. XVIII, in Kirch, "Enchiridion," 271.
34 Council of Elvira, Canon 32, in Kirch, "Enchiridion," 338.
35 Morinus, "De Poenitentiae Sacramento," VIII, xxiii, 1-11.

36 Council of Orange, Canon 3, Mansi, VI, 437.
37 Mansi, III, 951.
38 Council of Elvira, Canon 32, Kirch, "Enchiridion," 338.
39 Eusebius, "Hist. Eccl., VII, xvi, MPG. LXVII, 1459.
40 Eusebius, "Hist. Eccl.," IV, xix, MPG. LXVII, 614.
41 Clement of Rome, I Cor. LVII, 1, MPG. I, 323.
42 Homilia II, vi in Ps. XXXVII, 19, MPG. XII, 1386.
43 Pesch, "Institutiones Dogmaticae," VII, 497; Palmieri, "De Poenitentia," 514.
44 Morinus, "De Poenitentiae Sacramento," III, iv, 9.
45 St. Gregory Nazien., Serm. XXXIX, MPG. XXXVI, 355, 369.
46 Clement of Alex. in Eusebius, "Hist. Eccl.," III, xvii; St. Ambrose, "De Poenit," II, xx, MPL. XVI, 520; Der Katholik, 1885, 368.
47 MPG. I, 695.
48 Conc. Tridentinum, Sess. V, de peccato originali, Canon 5.
49 Eugene IV, Decretum pro Armenis, Denzinger-Bannwart, "Enchiridion," 696.
50 St. John Chrysostom, "Messis Quidem," V, MPG. LXIII, 522.
51 Dr. Schmitz, Der Katholik, 1885, 364.
52 Morinus, "De Poenitentiae Sacramento," III, iii, 11.
53 Paulus, "Geschichte des Ablasses im Mittelalter," I, 10.
54 Paulus, "Geschichte des Ablasses im Mittelalter," I, 10, note 4; "Les absolutions generelles, qui mettaient fin a la penitence canonique, avaient-elles quelque influence directe sur la dette des peches auxquels l'imposition de la penitence etait etrangers? Je ne vois aucune raison de la supposer."
55 Morinus, "De Poenitentiae Sacramento," III, i-iv; Der Katholik, 1885, 363 ff.
56 Der Katholik, 1885, 368.
57 Pesch, "Institutiones Dogmaticae," VII, 497; Palmieri, "De Poenitentia," 514.
58 Der Katholik, 1885, 365.
59 MPG. I, 695.
60 Der Katholik, 1885, 362.
61 Ordo Romanus, quoted by Schmitz, Der Katholik, 1885, 364.
62 Morinus, "De Poenitentiae Sacramento," Appendix, 44, 51, 60.
63 St. Cyprian, Ep. XVIII, Kirch, "Enchiridion," 271.
64 Council of Elvira, Canon 32, Kirch, "Enchiridion," 338.
65 Pesch, "Institutiones Dogmaticae," VII, 265, 410-416; Benedict XIV, "De Synodo Dioecesana," VII, xvi, 4.
66 Pesch, "Institutiones Dogmaticae," VII, 265.
67 Kirchenlexicon, art. "Bussdisciplin," II, 1569.
68 Morinus, "De Poenitentiae Sacramento," Appendix, 44, 51, 60.
69 Mansi, II, 515.
70 Mansi, II, 674.
71 Council of Elvira, Canon 32, Kirch, "Enchiridion," 338; St. Cyprian, Ep. XVIII, Kirch, 271.
72 St. Cyprian, Ep. XV, Kirch, "Enchiridion," 267.
73 Morinus, "De Poenitentiae Sacramento," Appendix, 20, 46.
74 Bellarmin, "De Indulgentiis et Jubilaeo Libri Duo," I, iii.
75 Der Katholik, 1885, 477. One can not but note a contradiction in the attitude of Dr. Schmitz. In the present instance, he ascribes the remission to perfect compliance with the enjoined penance, and not to reconciliation. Subsequently (Der Katholik, 1885, 489), speaking of the remission imparted on the occasion of presenting the "libelli martyrum," he says, directly contrariwise: "Die Form der Verleihung des Ablasses war die Ertheilung der feierlichen Reconciliation, welche wie in dem Falle der vom Buesser selbst geleisteten Busse, die Bedeutung eines vollkommenen, vor Got giltigen, Nachlasses der zeitlichen Suendenstrafen hatte."

76 Paulus, "Geschichte des Ablasses im Mittelalter," I, 8-10.
77 Der Katholik, 1885, 477, quoting St. Cyprian, Ep. IX, VII, LIII, LIX.
78 Der Katholik, 1885, 479.
79 Paulus, "Geschichte des Ablasses im Mittelalter," I, 10-11.
80 Ibidem, 9-11.
81 Mansi, II, 515.
82 Der Katholik, 1885, 483; Hilgers, "Die katholische Lehre von den Ablaessen und deren geschichtlichen Entwicklung," 45.
83 Eusebius, "Hist. Eccl," V, i, xl; Tertullian, "De Pudicit," XXII, MPL. II, 1027; Amort, "Histor. Indulg.," 28.
84 "De Pudicit," MPL. II, 1027.
85 Tertullian, "Ad Martyres," I, MPL. I, 621.
86 Particularly the practice of Pope Zephyrinus.
87 Ep. XVIII, Kirch, "Enchiridion," 271.
88 Ep. XVIII, Kirch, "Enchiridion," 271.
89 Paulus, "Geschichte des Ablasses im Mittelalter," I, 3.
90 De Lapsis, XVII, MPL. IV, 480.
91 De Lapsis, XVIII, MPL. IV, 480.
92 Ep. X, MPL. IV, 253-256.
93 Ep. XXI, MPL. IV, 279.
94 Cf. above, 6.
95 De Pudicit, XXII, MPL. II, 1026.
96 Bellarmin, "De Indul. et Jubil. Libri Duo," I, iii.
97 Otten, "Manual," II, 363; Hilgers, "Die kath. Lehre von den Abl. und deren gesch. Entwicklung," 50 ff.
98 Paulus, "Geschichte des Ablasses im Mittelalter," I, 11.
99 Mansi, II, 529.
100 Mansi, II, 530.
101 Mansi, II, 674.
102 Council of Elvira, Canon 63, Mansi, II, 115.
103 Mansi, II, 519.
104 Mansi, II, 522.
105 Paulus, "Geschichte des Ablasses im Mittelalter," I, 11.
106 Morinus, "De Poenitentiae Sacramento," X, xvii, 3: "Verae poenitentiae actae canonice fructus est, et optimi poenitentis vehementissime contriti argumentum."
107 Ep. CLIX, MPL. LIV, 1138.
108 Ad Amphilochium, MPG. XXXII, 803.
109 Hilgers, "Die kath. Lehre von den Abl. und deren gesch. Entwicklung," XXIX.
110 Reuter-Lehmkuhl, "Neo-Confessarius," VI, xviii, 3.
111 Paulus, "Geschichte des Ablasses im Mittelalter," I, 12.
112 Morinus, "De Poenitentiae Sacramento," X, xvii, 4; Paulus, "Geschichte des Ablasses im Mittelalter," I, 13.
113 Der Katholik, 1885, 628.
114 Der Katholik, 1885, 628-629.
115 Der Katholik, 1885, 630; Morinus, "De Poenitentiae Sacramento," X, xvii, 5.
116 Mansi, XII, 403.
117 Mansi, XIV, 102.
118 Mansi, XIV, 554; Der Katholik, 1885, 631.
119 Mansi, XIV, 904.
120 Der Katholik, 1885, 632.
121 Der Katholik, 1885, 632.
122 Mansi, XVIII A, 160.
123 Mansi, XVIII A, 162.
124 Paulus, "Geschichte des Ablasses im Mittelalter," I, 14.

125 Mansi, XIX, 893.
126 Morinus, "De Poenitentiae Sacramento," X, xvi, xvii, xviii.
127 Paulus, "Geschichte des Ablasses im Mittelalter," I, 12.
128 Der Katholik, 1885, 629.
129 Der Katholik, 1885, 629.
130 Hilger's "Die kath. Lehre von den Abl. und deren gesch. Entwicklung," XXIX.
131 Paulus, "Geschichte des Ablasses im Mittelalter," I, 20, note 5.
132 Paulus, "Geschichte," etc., I, 21, text and note 2.
133 Paulus, "Geschichte," etc., I, 20.
134 Der Katholik, 1885, 633, citing the action of St. Boniface.
135 Der Katholik, 1885, 633.
136 Der Katholik, 1885, 634.
137 Morinus, "De Poenitentiae Sacramento," VIII, ix, 5.
138 MPL. CXLV, 1405.
139 Paulus, "Geschichte," etc., I, 24.
140 MPL. CXXVI, 743.
141 MPL. CXXIX, 807.
142 MPL. CXXVI, 1048.
143 C. 1, de poenit. et remiss. V, 9, in Extravag. com.
144 Conc. Trident. Sess., XXV, de reform., Contin. Sess., Decretum de indulgentiis.
145 Paulus, "Geschichte," etc., I, 24.
146 Paulus, "Geschichte," etc., I, 15, quoting Harnack: "Die Entstehung der Ablaesse wurzelt in der Praxis der Redemptionen."
147 Paulus, "Geschichte," etc., I, 135-136.
148 Paulus, "Geschichte," etc., I, 137-138; ZKT. XXXIII, 3.
149 ZKT. XXXIII, 15.
150 ZKT. XXXIII, 6.
151 Paulus, "Geschichte," etc., I, 142.
152 Paulus, "Geschichte," etc., I, 143.
153 ZKT. XXXIII, 6.
154 Paulus, "Geschichte," etc., II, 60.
155 C. 12, X, de excessibus praelatorum et subditorum, V, 31.
156 Paulus, "Geschichte," etc., I, 147. St. Thomas' statement (In IV Sent. dis. 20, quest. 1, art. 5) that Gregory the Great granted a seven years' indulgence for the Stations of Rome is an historical error of the Angelic Doctor. The comment of Natalis Alexander on another historical error of St. Thomas applies to the present case: "Quod S. Thomae institutum non fuit expendere quaestiones chronologicas et historicas, unde pronum fuit, ut a vera temporum et historiae relatione recederit." Amort, "Historia Indul.," I, i, 42, 46.
157 Pflugk-Harttung, "Acta Pont. Rom. Inedita," III, 2.
158 Paulus, "Geschichte," etc., I, 141.
159 Paulus, "Geschichte," etc., I, 141.
160 Paulus, "Geschichte," etc., I, 147.
161 Paulus, "Geschichte," etc., I, 148.
162 Paulus, "Geschichte," etc., I, 148.
163 Paulus, "Geschichte," etc., I, 148.
164 Amort, "Historia Indul.," I, i, 46.
165 Paulus, "Geschichte," etc., I, 151.
166 Giorgi-Balzani, "Il Regesto di Farfa di Gregorio di Catino," V, 291.
167 Paulus, "Geschichte," etc., I, 151.
168 Paulus, "Geschichte," etc., I, 152.
169 Paulus, "Geschichte," etc., I, 153
170 MPL. CLI, 448; CLXXI, 749.
171 Amort, "Historia Indul," I, i, 45.

172 Paulus, "Geschichte," etc., I, 39-57.
173 Paulus, "Geschichte," etc., I, 195.
174 Mansi, XX, 816.
175 Amort, "Historia Indul.," I, ii, 2-91.
176 Herbert Thurston, S. J. The Month, LXXXXIX, 429.
177 C. 1, de poenit. et remiss., V, 9, in Extravag. com.
178 The Month, LXXXXIX, 429.
179 Cf. above, 30.
180 MPL. CCXV, 1470, 1356.
181 MPL. LXXXII, 322.
182 C. 1, de poenit. et remiss., V, 9, in Extravag. com.
183 C. 2, de poenit. et remiss., V, 9, in Extravag. com.
184 C. 4, de poenit. et remiss., V, 9, in Extravag. com.

CHAPTER III.

AN ANALYSIS OF CANON 911.

As previously remarked, the definition that is to serve us as norm in this dissertation is that contained in Canon 911 of the Code: "Let all highly prize indulgences, or the remission before God of the temporal punishment due to sins already forgiven as to guilt, which remission the ecclesiastical authority grants out of the treasure of the Church, and applies to the living by way of absolution, to the departed by way of suffrage."

To serve clearness, it is well to distinguish in this definition two sets of elements, namely, those which belong to the essence of the idea, and those which are merely explanatory. To the latter class belong (A) the utility of indulgences (Omnes magni faciant), (B) the manner of their application to the living (Pro vivis per modum absolutionis), (C) their applicability to the departed (Pro defunctis per modum suffragii). Concerning each of these points a few words will be said after a disposal has been made of the several essential factors of the definition, towit: I. the negative element (Non culpae), II. the positive element (Remissio poenae temporalis debitae pro peccatis), III. the value of indulgences (Coram Deo), IV. their source (Ex thesauro Ecclesiae), and V. the authority that gives them currency (Ecclesiastica auctoritas). These factors will now be discussed in order.

A. THE ESSENTIAL NOTES IN THE DEFINITION OF CANON 911.

I. The Negative Element (Non Culpae.)

Every sin inflicts on the soul a two-fold wound, and the distinction between these two wounds must ever be borne in mind in considering the remission which an indulgence imparts. There is, first of all, the wound of guilt, of which the theologians speak as the "reatus culpae." This consists in the turning away from God and the conversion to creatures. Consequent to this is the forfeiture, either entire or partial, of the divine friendship. The perpetrator of mortal sin turns completely away from God, utterly forfeits the divine friendship and therefore incurs spiritual death. On the other hand, the commission of venial sin, being only a diminution of our allegiance to God and a partial conversion to creatures, does not entirely deprive the soul of the divine complacency, so that the venial sinner's wound of guilt is not a wound to death.[1]

But besides the guilt of sin, though inevitably connected with it, there is the so-called "reatus poenae," or liability to punishment. Every sin is a detraction from the honor due to God; it withholds from Him that fealty and obedience of ours to which He has an indisputable claim. St. Thomas, in placing the chief constituent of mortal sin in the aversion from God, and the principal element of venial sin in the conversion to creatures, argues that mortal sin deserves an eternal punishment, as being a complete rebellion against God, but that the punishment due to venial sin is only temporary, since venial sin lacks the factor of absolute rebellion, and consists merely in an inordinate complacency with creatures, which complacency does not constitute an infinite offense.[2] Moreover, since mortal sin contains both the element of rebellion and the subordinate element of conversion to creatures, it merits, besides the eternal punishment, also a temporal punishment akin to that visited upon venial sin. Thus St. Thomas concludes.[3]

There arises the question of healing these two wounds inflicted on the soul by sin. For the healing of the deathly wound of guilt inflicted by mortal sin, Christ instituted the Sacrament of Penance. Reception of this Sacrament, or when the actual reception of it is impossible, an act of perfect contrition with the resolve to confess, heals the wound of guilt and restores the soul to divine favor. And since the state of sanctifying grace thus restored in Confession is incompatible with liability to eternal punishment, the pardon of guilt imparted by Confession necessarily brings with it the cancellation of the eternal penalty due to sin.

Concerning the forgiveness of the guilt of venial sin, the Council of Trent teaches that although it is proper and useful to confess venial sins, there are many other ways by which these can be forgiven.[4] Of the ways in which the guilt of venial sins is forgiven outside Confession, the most generally mentioned are: acts of contrition and attrition, hearing Mass, receiving Holy Communion, and the devout use of the Sacramentals.[5]

From the preceding paragraphs it is easy to deduce the meaning of the negative element in the definition of indulgences: "ad culpam quod attinet jam deletis."[6] Indulgences are not to be enumerated among the means whereby the forgiveness of the guilt of any sin is to be obtained. The guilt or offense contained in any sin whatsoever must have been previously removed—by Confession or perfect contrition cum voto, in the case of mortal sin; by these, or by one of the other prescribed means, in the case of venial sin—before there can be question of the removal of the temporal punishment due to these sins, through the medium of indulgences.[7]

But if an indulgence does not imply the remission of the guilt of sin, how is one to understand some of the older formularies of the Church, in which indulgences were granted from sin, no distinction being made between the guilt and the penalty thereof? A case in point is the publication of the first Jubilee Indulgence by Boniface VIII: "Antiquorum habet fida relatio quod concessae sunt magnae remissiones et indulgentiae peccatorum. Nos—hujusmodi indulgentias—apostolica auctoritate confirmamus."[8] The terminology of this particular formulary offers no special difficulty, for a gloss of the Corpus Juris has added a marginal note to "peccatorum," explaining: "id est, poenarum pro peccatis debitarum."[9] This explanation of the glossator may be extended to all instances in which the expression "indulgentia peccatorum" occurs. In Holy Scripture, as well as in the early ecclesiastical writers, "peccatum" or sin was the generic term applied without distinction to guilt, penalty, and atonement of sin. In the celebrated passage from Machabees: "It is a holy and wholesome thought to pray for the dead that they may be loosed from their sins,"[10] "sins" most manifestly refers, not to the guilt of sin, but to the temporal penalty, since after death there is no forgiveness of guilt. Again, when St. Paul says of Christ: "Him who knew no sin, He hath made sin for us,"[11] he uses "sin" in the meaning of victim or atonement for sin. St. Augustine blames certain heretics of his day for having ignored these various meanings of "sin" in the Scriptures.[12] And the same reproach may be directed against those who argue from the terminology of certain formularies that indulgences purport to be a remission of the guilt of sin. In using the expression "indulgentia peccatorum" the composers of such formularies were merely conforming to ancient linguistic usage, as both the context of each of these formularies and the pertinent, contemporary teaching reveal.

A similar difficulty is met where indulgences are granted "from guilt and punishment" (a culpa et a poena). Regarding this formula, Benedict XIV remarks that it was used by pre-Reformation preachers of indulgence, and that it was the occasion of many bitter attacks against the whole doctrine of indulgences. He cites a passage from Clement V [13] to prove that even the use of this formula, and much more the implication that indulgences were a pardon of both guilt and punishment, was reprobated by the Pope. The passage from Clement V voices a condemnation of certain preachers who, on the occasion of announcing an indulgence, collected sums of money. Among other things, the following occurs: "They grant a plenary remission of sins, and some of them absolve from penalty and from guilt (to use their words); desirous of completely abolishing such abuses through which the power of the keys and the authority of the Church are brought into contempt, we decree, etc." From the parenthetic insertion, "to use their words," Pope Benedict argues: "The Pope (i.e., Clement V) clearly shows that this manner of speaking was wholly incongruous."[14]

Suarez admits that some Popes granted indulgences "a culpa et a poena," particularly Jubilee Indulgences. He explains them as meaning that the gainer of such an indulgence is absolved from both guilt and penalty, not because the indulgence produces both these effects, but because, in order to have its full effect, such an indulgence presupposes the remission of all guilt; the indulgence, remitting all penalty, complements the remission of guilt previously obtained.[15] Suarez also refers to the opinion of some that these words "a culpa et a poena" not only conceded an indulgence, but that "a poena" meant that faculties were granted for absolving from all sins, even sins that were ordinarily reserved. This explanation of the import of "a culpa" gains weight from the consideration that indulgences a "poena et a culpa" were usually Jubilee Indulgences, and at the time of Jubilee it was and still is customary to concede very ample faculties for absolving from reserved cases.[16] So, whatever be the correct explanation, whether the form "a culpa et a poena" was ever sanctioned by papal use or not, that form was never meant to imply that an indulgence entailed the remission of the guilt of sin, but only of the punishment. Incidentally, the Council of Constance in 1417 revoked all indulgences, by whomsoever granted, in which occurred the formula "a culpa et a poena," or its equivalent, "in plena remissione."[17]

II. The Positive Element (Remissio Poenae Temporalis Pro Peccatis).

A previous paragraph treated the remission of the eternal punishment which mortal sin deserves. It now remains to discuss the discharge of the temporal punishment due to venial sin, and also that part of the penalty for mortal sin which is but temporal. It is possible, in fact, it actually happens, that the pardon of sin is sometimes complete, embracing not only the remission of guilt and the eternal punishment, but also of all temporal punishment as well. Christ's pardon of the thief on the Cross was of this character. For the Redeemer's assurance: "Amen, I say unto you, this day thou shalt be with me in paradise,"[18] clearly implied the complete cancellation of even the temporal punishment due to the penitent's sins. Again, in adult Baptism, every vestige of sin is removed from the soul, so that, according to the teaching of the Council of Trent, there is nothing odious to God in the souls of those just baptized, nothing at all to prevent their immediate entrance into heaven.[19]

But the pardon of the guilt of sin does not necessarily include remission of all the temporal punishment due thereto. Quite the reverse, as a rule, some temporal punishment remains to be expiated even after the entire guilt has been condoned by God. This, too, is the doctrine of Trent: "The Holy Synod declares that it is entirely false and contrary to the word of God that guilt is never pardoned by God unless all penalty is also pardoned."[20] "If anyone say that the entire penalty is always remitted by God along with the guilt,—let him be anathema."[21] "If anyone say that it is a fiction that, when the eternal punishment has been removed by the power of the keys, the temporal penalty generally remains to be paid, let him be anathema."[22]

Before the soul may enter heaven, the debt of temporal punishment must be paid. And it is paid in one of two ways, either by satispassion or by satisfaction. Satispassion consists in undergoing the hardships to which we are subject in this life, as expiatory sufferings, or in the atonements exacted in Purgatory. On the other hand, satisfaction means the substitution of something acceptable to God in lieu of the punishment we should otherwise have to undergo. Prayers, alms, works of mercy and charity, virtuous deeds in general, tend to satisfy for our temporal debt. "Habemus plura subsidia quibus peccata nostra redimamus. Pecuniam habes, redime peccatum tuum," says St. Ambrose;[23] and the Prophet Daniel: "Peccata tua eleemosynis redime.''[24] Over and above these, there is a class of works on which the Church has set her stamp, affixing to them a specific satisfactory or expiatory value. And these condonations officially granted by the Church are called indulgences.

III. The Value of Indulgences (*Coram Deo*).

It may be asked: What weight attaches to such remissions granted by the Church? The answer is given in the third element of the definition of Canon 911: ''An indulgence is a remission before God.'' Martin Luther contended, and the contention was later reiterated by the pseudo-synod of Pistoia, that indulgences are in no sense a remission of that punishment which the divine justice exacts, but are at best nothing more than a relaxation of the penitential discipline, a retrenchment from the rigorous penances imposed by the early Church. Indulgences, therefore, in the minds of these heretics, had weight before the Church, but were of no value before God. Luther's error, condemned by the Bull ''Exsurge Domine'' of Leo X, was couched in the following terms: ''Even in the case of those who actually gain them, indulgences do not effect the remission of punishments due to sin before the divine justice.''[25] In condemning the error of the Synod of Pistoia: ''According to its precise notion, an indulgence is nothing more than the remission of part of the penance imposed for sins by the canons,''[26] Pius VI, in the Bull ''Auctorem Fidei,'' declared this proposition ''False, temerarious, injurious to the merits of Christ, already condemned in the nineteenth article of Luther.''[27] The condemnation of these two propositions proves that the mind of the Church in granting indulgences is to grant a remission of temporal punishment that is ratified by God; to exercise, in one respect, the power imparted to her in the commission of Christ: "Whatsoever you shall loose upon earth shall be loosed also in heaven."[28] And certainly, if indulgences were no more than the relaxation of the rigor of ancient penitential canons, the power of granting them had long since become illusory. For in other ways the rigor of penitential discipline has been so modified that there can be no need of a peculiar power vested in the Church to effect further modification of that which has already become extremely lenient. Therefore, if the remission granted by indulgences is to mean anything, it must mean a remission which is valid in the sight of God.

IV. Source of Efficacy of Indulgences (Ex Thesauro Ecclesiae).

Allusion has been made above to the fact that satisfaction for temporal punishment, and hence indulgences, does not imply an outright cancellation of that punishment, but rather the substitution of something in its stead. As St. Thomas puts it: "He who receives an indulgence is not absolved, strictly speaking, from the debt of punishment, but there is given him something wherewith to make payment."[29] Now, on what source does the Church draw for the satisfactions tendered in the case of indulgences? Canon 911 gives the answer, saying: "The ecclesiastical authority grants indulgences out of the treasury of the Church." The Church possesses an inexhaustible storehouse of satisfactions. And each indulgence that she grants withdraws some part of the wealth there stored, and places it at the disposal of him who gains the indulgence. This he may offer to God in lieu of the actual endurance of the temporal punishment which he owes.

To understand the nature of this treasury of the Church—the doctrine of which was first adequately explained by Alexander of Hales—it is necessary to outline in brief some of the truths on which the existence of such a treasure depends. These are, principally: the manifold value of good works, vicarious satisfaction, the Communion of Saints, and the superabundance of the satisfaction of the Saints and of Christ.

Every good work of the just possesses at least a twofold value: the value of merit, whereby it entitles the doer to a reward, and the value of satisfaction, whereby it atones for past transgressions. Both of these values are clearly indicated in the Scriptures. Perhaps the most conspicuous testimony to the meritorious character of good works is contained in the passage from St. Matthew, wherein our Lord represents the kingdom of heaven as a reward for the deeds of the just: "Come—possess you the kingdom prepared for you—. For I was hungry and you gave me to eat, etc."[31] The satisfactory quality of good works is indicated in the Old Testament passage: "Water quencheth a flaming fire, and alms resisteth sins."[32] The same is true of the text of Daniel: "Redeem thou thy sins with alms, and thy iniquities with works of mercy to the poor."[33] What is here said specifically of alms applies with equal force to the spiritual and corporal works of mercy, prayer, fasting, and other forms of good works.

The meritorious value of our good works is not transferable. Each merits for himself alone: "Every man shall receive his own reward according to his own labor."[34] There can be no vicarious merit. On the other hand, there is vicarious satisfaction, that is, the offering of one person's satisfactions in payment for another's debt of punishment.[35]

It is in the Communion of Saints that the possibility of the exchange of satisfaction is most completely realized. In virtue of the intimate union existing between the members of Christ's mystical Body, one member aids the other, even as the parts of our physical bodies lend mutual assistance. It is as members of this Communion of Saints, as exchangers of satisfactions, that St. Paul admonishes the Galatians: "Bear ye one another's burdens."[36] The reciprocation of benefits in the Communion of Saints is not limited to the offering of prayers in behalf of each other, but likewise embraces an actual exchange of the satisfactory fruits of good works.

Keeping in mind the truths of vicarious satisfaction and the Communion of Saints, it is easier to arrive at a more definite understanding of what the phrase "treasure of the Church" means. In that treasury are stored, first by reason of their dignity and abundance, the infinite satisfactions of our Saviour. By reason of the hypostatic union, the least act of Christ was of infinite value, capable of satisfying the divine justice for the sins of the world. The unnumbered hardships and cruel tortures and ignominious death which He underwent were superabundant. But they were not wasted. The wisdom of God forbids that satisfactions so precious should be turned to no account. They were stored away, so to speak, for future emergencies, to be applied at a later time in expiation of the penalties due to the sins of generations to come.[37]

In addition to these infinite satisfactions of Christ, the treasure of the Church includes the abundant satisfactions of the Blessed Mother of God and those of the Saints. For the Mother of our Lord, preserved as she was from all taint of sin, had no need of performing works expiatory of penalties due to sin. Yet perform them she did, in great number and with the most perfect dispositions. Many Saints of God, while leading lives of innocence, nevertheless underwent rigorous forms of self-discipline and self-abnegation, works of their very nature satisfactory for sins. These satisfactions were added to those of Christ. The Church has consistently recognized this treasure. And when Luther impiously denied its existence, his error was forthwith condemned.[38] Pius VI condemned as "false, temerarious, injurious to the merits of Christ and the Saints," the proposition of the Synod of Pistoia, asserting that the Scholastics by their subtleties had invented a treasury of merits of Christ and the Saints, and had replaced the clear notion of absolution from canonical penance with the confused idea of an application of merits.[39]

V. The Authorization of Indulgences (Ecclesiastica Auctoritas).

The disposal of this rich treasure has been entrusted to the authority of the Catholic Church; "Indulgentias —ecclesiastica auctoritas concedit"[40]. The power to grant indulgences is but one phase of the power given to the Church "to bind and to loose," the power of the keys. The giving of the keys of the kingdom of heaven conferred on the Church the prerogative of opening heaven to souls. "Whatsoever you shall loose on earth" contained no exception; it included the power of loosing from guilt, and a fortiori, from penalty. By the power of the keys the Church has been charged to remove whatever impedes souls from entering heaven, be it guilt or penalty. Accordingly, we find the Council of Trent declaring: "Since the power of granting indulgences was conferred on the Church by Christ, and since from most ancient times she has used this divinely bestowed power, the Holy Synod anathematizes those who deny that the power of granting indulgences is in the Church."[41] Also the confession of faith of Pius VI states: "I affirm that the power of granting indulgences was left in the Church."[42]

Being one aspect of the power of the keys, the granting of indulgences for the faithful is an act of jurisdiction. Therefore it is to be exercised by the ecclesiastical authority to whom Christ has committed jurisdiction over the faithful, to whose keeping has been entrusted the wealth of the Church.[43] Further reference to those whom "ecclesiastica auctoritas" embraces will be made in a later chapter.

B. NOTES EXPLANATORY OF CANON 911.

We return now to discuss those elements which were mentioned above as being explanatory of the definition given in Canon 911, namely, the utility of indulgences, the manner of their application to the living, their applicability to the dead.

I. The Utility of Indulgences (Omnes Magni Faciant Indulgentias).

"Let all highly prize indulgences" is the injunction of Canon 911 in reference to the usefulness of indulgences. And the reason why indulgences are to be made much of is contained in the dogmatic definition of the Council of Trent: "The Holy Synod teaches that the use of indulgences is highly salutary to the Christian people—and it anathematizes those who assert that they are useless."[44] It is because they are useful and very beneficial to the faithful that indulgences are to be held in high esteem. Luther had asserted that indulgences were not expedient, that they were pious frauds, that those were deceived who believed that indulgences were of any spiritual benefit.[45] The condemnation of Luther's errors, the teaching of the Tridentine Synod, and the exhortation of Canon 911 all combine to prove the solicitude which the Church has for inculcating in the faithful the highest regard for this efficacious means of succoring both the living and the dead.

II. The Applicability to the Living (Vivis per Modum Absolutionis).

There is a distinction between the manner in which indulgences are applied to the living and their applicability to the departed.[46] So far as the living are concerned, indulgences partake of the nature of a juridical absolution. The living members of the Church are subjects of the Church's jurisdiction, subjects of the power of the keys. And every indulgence granted to the living is simply an exercise of that power of juridically absolving subjects capable of absolution. Hence the efficacy of an indulgence applied to a living subject who, with the right dispositions, has complied with the requirements, is certain, infallible. The remission of temporal punishment, in whole or in part, is directly and certainly applied to the rightly disposed, even as the remission of guilt is directly and infallibly imparted to the rightly disposed in the Sacrament of Penance.

While it is true that indulgences are granted to the living by way of absolution, still the remission differs from sacramental absolution imparted in the tribunal of Penance insofar as the indulgence does not simply remit the punishment. Instead, it pays off the debt of penalty by offering up to God a portion of the Church's spiritual wealth. Hence St. Bonaventure says: "This relaxation, or the granting of an indulgence implies two things, namely, the communication of the treasure of the Church, and together with this a certain juridical absolution.''[47]

III. Application to the Dead (Defunctis per Modum Suffragii).

If the doctrine of indulgences for the living has been attacked, much more vehement have been the attacks made on indulgences for the dead. In enumerating the six classes for whom indulgences were neither necessary nor useful, Luther mentions the dead in the first place.[48] With a similar spirit the recalcitrant Synod of Pistoia asserted: ''It is even more to be deprecated that they have attempted to transfer this chimerical application (sc. of the merits of Christ and the Saints) to the dead.''[49] Besides condemning this error and the kindred error of Peter of Osma ''The Pope cannot grant anyone an indulgence of the punishment of Purgatory,''[50] the Church, at least since the thirteenth century [50a] practiced the application of indulgences to the dead. The legitimacy of that practice appears from this that it were impossible for the Church, under the guidance of the Holy Ghost, to have erred thus grievously in a moral matter of such grave importance.[51] Moreover, there is no cogent reason why the souls in Purgatory should be excluded from the benefits of the treasure of the Church. For they still belong to the Communion of Saints and are members of Christ's mystical Body.[52] Moveover, it is the souls in Purgatory who stand in greatest need of indulgences for it is they, in the words of Sixtus IV, who cannot help themselves, and therefore most sorely need the suffrages of others.[53] Indeed, the whole power of granting indulgences would be in a great measure illusory if it could not reach the departed. Again, in Pope Leo X's defense of the Church's power to grant indulgences, both the living and the dead are declared the beneficiaries of that power: "By these letters we wish to make known to you that the Roman Church, drawing upon the superabundance of the merits of Christ and the Saints, can grant indulgences to the faithful in Christ, whether in this life or in Purgatory, and that in granting indulgences both to the living and the dead by apostolic authority, she is wont to dispense her treasure, conferring the indulgence by way of absolution, or transferring it by way of suffrage."[54]

From the concluding words of the passage just quoted from Pope Leo X it appears that indulgences are applicable to the souls of the departed, not in the form of absolution, but only by way of suffrage. That is to say, the indulgences applied to the dead do not directly remit their punishments. But the Church, as it were, takes from her treasure a portion corresponding to the terms of the indulgence, and offers that portion of satisfactions to God, begging Him to reduce proportionately the penalties of the poor souls. This taking of satisfactions from her treasure and offering them to God the Church does only on condition that the works prescribed for gaining the indulgence be performed by someone among the living. The penalties of the poor souls are remitted only if the conditions are fulfilled; there is no gratuitous cancellation.[55] Gaining an indulgence for the dead, therefore, means performing the prescribed works, in view of which the Church entreats God to accept the indulgence on behalf of the departed.

The expression "by way of suffrage" may appear to reduce indulgences for the dead to the level of ordinary prayers in their behalf. But this is not the meaning intended by the phrase. Suffrage, in the present instance, means more than intercession. It means a plea supported by the offering of the satisfactions of Christ and the Saints. In explaining the term, Pope Sixtus IV declared that though it was customary to speak of alms, good works and non-indulgenced prayers offered for the suffering souls as suffrages, still, there is a wide difference between all works of this class and indulgences granted by way of suffrage. Such alms and deeds of charity have in common with indulgences, not the same measure of efficacy, but only the manner of operation; they are all similar only in this respect that all operate as suffrages; they are dissimilar so far as their effects are concerned.[56]

Since indulgences for the dead operate as suffrages, their effect is not infallible. Acceptance of them depends on God's free will. God has in no wise obligated Himself to accept them at their face value. Neither has He assumed any obligation of accepting them in behalf of the particular soul for whom they have been offered. Therefore the Church has never disapproved, but has always encouraged the practice of the faithful gaining numerous indulgences, plenary as well as partial, for one and the same departed soul. This fact was in the mind of the Congregation of Indulgences when, in answer to the question: "Whether by the indulgence attached to a privileged altar is to be understood a plenary indulgence immediately freeing the soul from all penalties of Purgatory, or only an indulgence to be applied according to the pleasure of the divine mercy?" the Congregation said: "If we consider the will of the granter and the power of the keys, a plenary indulgence is here to be understood which would at once free the soul from all the pains of Purgatory; but if we consider the effects of the application, an indulgence is to be understood which corresponds in measure to the wish of the divine mercy."[57] What is here said of the indulgence of the privileged altar applies to all indulgences of the dead: so far as depends on the mind of the Church and the power of the Church in the disposal of the treasure of satisfactions, those indulgences are certainly productive of the stated remission: "tantum valent quantum sonant"; but so far as their acceptance by God is concerned, they are subject to the same possibilities as a prayer, albeit a prayer backed by the satisfactions of Christ. Their precise value, so far as acceptance by God is concerned, is known only to Divine Providence.

But what, after all, is the basis for this discrimination against the faithful departed? If they are members of the Communion of Saints, and are entitled to the benefit of one of the chief goods of that Communion, namely, its wealth of satisfactions; if, moreover, they stand in sorest need of those satisfactions, then why should they be denied access to that treasure on equal terms with the living? Why may they not be subjects of indulgence "per modum absolutionis"? The reason is that death has removed them from the jurisdiction of the Church. Whereas the living are subject to divine jurisdiction through the mediation of the Church, the status of the departed is altered, and they are immediately subject to divine jurisdiction, without the mediumship of the Church. Now, absolution can be given to none except subjects; the faithful departed are not subjects of the Church; therefore indulgences cannot be imparted to them by way of absotion, but only by way of suffrage, in the manner described above.

NOTES ON CHAPTER III.

1 Beringer-Hilgers, "Die Ablaesse," I, 2.
2 St. Thomas, Summa Theologica, III, q. 84, art. 4.
3 St. Thomas, Summa Theologica, III, q. 84, art. 4.
4 Conc. Trident., sess. XIV, de Poenitentia, c. 5.
5 Wilmers, "Lehrbuch der Religion," IV, 97.
6 Canon 911.
7 Benedict XIV, "De Synodo Dioecesana," XIII, xiii, 7.
8 Cap. 1, Antiquorum, V, 9, in Extravag. com.
9 Cap. 1, Antiquorum, V, 9, in Extravag. com.
10 II Mach., XII, 46.
11 II Cor., V, 21.
12 MPL. XLIV, 598.
13 Cap. 2, de poenitentiis et remissionibus, V, 9, in Clementinis.
14 Benedict XIV, "De Synodo Dioecesana," XIII, xviii, 7.
15 De Sacramentis, II, disp. 50, sec. 1.
16 Paulus, "Geschichte des Ablasses im Mittelalter," II, 137.
17 Beringer-Hilgers, "Die Ablaesse," I, 17.
18 Luke, XXIII, 43.
19 Conc. Trident., sess. V, de peccato originali, can. 5.
20 Conc. Trident., sess. XIV, de poenitentia, cap. 8.
21 Conc. Trident., sess. XIV, de poenitentia, can. 12
22 Conc. Trident., sess. XIV, de poenitentia, can. 15.
23 MPL. XIV, 724.
24 Daniel, IV, 24.
25 Denzinger-Bannwart, "Enchiridion," 759.
26 Denzinger-Bannwart, "Enchiridion," 1540.
27 Denzinger-Bannwart, "Enchiridion," 1540.
28 Matthew, XVIII, 18.
29 St. Thomas, Summa Theologica, Suppl., q. 25, art. 1, ad 2um.
30 Paulus, "Geschichte des Ablasses im Mittelalter," II, 184.
31 Matthew, XXV, 34-36.
32 Ecclus., III, 33.
33 Daniel, IV, 24.
34 I Cor., III, 8.
35 Roman Catechism, "Penance," c. 5, q. 61; St. Thomas, Quodlibeta, II, q. 8, art. 16.
36 Galatians, VI, 2.
37 Cap. 2, de poenitentiis et remissionibus, V, 9, in Extravag. com.
38 Denzinger-Bannwart, "Enchiridion," 757.
39 Denzinger-Bannwart, "Enchiridion," 1541.
40 Canon 911.
41 Conc. Trident., sess. XXV, Decretum de indulgentiis.
42 Cavallera, "Thesaurus Doctrinae Catholicae," 1271.
43 Cap. 2, de poenitentiis et remissionibus, V, 9, in Extravag. com.
44 Conc. Trident., sess. XXV, Decretum de indulgentiis.
45 Cavallera, "Thesaurus Doctrinae Catholicae," 1270.
46 Canon 911.
47 In Quattuor Sententias, Dist. 20, pars. 2, art. 1, q. 5.
48 Denzinger-Bannwart, "Enchiridion," 762.
49 Denzinger-Bannwart, "Enchiridion," 1542.
50 Denzinger-Bannwart, "Enchiridion," 729.
50a Paulus, "Geschichte des Ablasses in Mittelalter," II, 160.
51 Theodore de Spiritu Sancto, quoted in Beringer-Hilgers, "Die Ablaesse," I, 96.
52 MPL. XLI, 674.
53 Cavallera, "Thesaurus Doctrinae Catholicae," 1264.

54 Cavallera, "Thesaurus Doctrinae Catholicae," 1266.

55 Beringer-Hilgers, "Die Ablaesse," I, 99.

56 "Non enim nos declaravimus—supradictam indulgentiam plenariam animabus in purgatorio existentibus, ac si fierent pro eisdem devotae orationes—videri prodesse, non quod intenderemus, prout nec intendimus—indulgentiam non plus proficere aut valere quam eleemosyna et orationes, aut eleemosynas tantum valere tantumque proficere quantum indulgentia per modum suffragii, cum sciamus orationes et eleemosynas et indulgentiam per modum suffragii longe distare, sed perinde valere diximus, id est per eum modum, per ac si, id est, per quem orationes et eleemosynae valent." Cavallera, "Thesaurus Doctrinae Catholicae," 1265.

57 Decr. Auth. S. C. Indul. et Reliq., 283.

CHAPTER IV.

The Division of Indulgences.

In essentials all indulgences are alike, since all partake of the characteristics noted in the preceding chapter. Accidentally, however, there are differences among indulgences, which differences give rise to a manifold division.

A. By reason of the effect produced indulgences may be: (a) plenary, or (b) partial. The former, as the name indicates, is a full remission of all the temporal punishment owed by the person to whom the indulgence is applied. A partial indulgence remits only a portion of that punishment.

Certain terms often added to the adjectives "plenary" and "partial" require notice here, as do also some concepts involved in plenary and partial indulgences. Plenary indulgence is often modified by the adjective "quotidiana perpetua" or "quotidiana ad tempus." This modification is especially frequent in the case of those indulgences granted for visiting churches. These expressions seem to imply that an indulgence so modified is to be gained on every day of the year. However, a response of the Congregation of Indulgences [1] determined that, unless the rescript in which the indulgence was granted specifically provided otherwise, an "indulgentia quotidiana" was to be gained but once a year. The Code adopts this decision, clarifying it somewhat by adding that the work to which the indulgence is attached may be performed on any day of the year one chooses.[2] Another modification of the plenary indulgence is made by the phrase "toties quoties" the meaning of which is that the indulgence thus modified may be gained as often as the conditions enjoined are fulfilled, even repeatedly on one and the same day. Perhaps the best known toties quoties indulgence is that of the Portiuncula, to be gained as often as one visits a church of the Franciscans on the second of August. The toties quoties indulgence is an illustration of a particular concession which Canon Law admits in contravention of the general rule that only one plenary indulgence attached to a particular work may be gained on the same day, though the work be repeated.[3]

The gaining of a plenary indulgence as such is not an easy matter. For in defining indulgences, Canon 911 says that an indulgence is the remission of the temporal punishment due to sins *the guilt of which has already been forgiven.* That is to say, the temporal punishment due to any sin cannot be remitted until that sin has been forgiven as to its guilt.[3a] The soul on which rests the guilt of the slightest venial sin cannot receive a complete remission of all temporal punishment, or a plenary indulgence as such or "plenario modo," for that unforgiven venial sin impedes the plenary indulgence from having its full effect.

But is the entire effect of the plenary indulgence lost for him who places in its way the obstacle of a venial sin? Does the soul in venial sin receive no remission from all the plenary indulgences it strives to gain? Formerly this contingency was met by the device of granting the indulgence in some such form as "plenary, and a specified number (7, 50, 100) of years." Then those whom the obstacle of an unforgiven venial sin excluded from the boon of a plenary indulgence, certainly gained the alternative, partial indulgence.[4] The Code meets the situation thus: "It is to be understood that a plenary indulgence is granted in such a way that if one cannot gain it in plenary form, nevertheless one gains it partially according to the dispositions one has."[5] The precise extent of "partially" in this connection cannot be fixed. Vermeersch explains it as meaning a remission of all punishment save the penalty due to the venial sin, the guilt of which has not been remitted.[6] This explanation accords with the opinion which St. Alphonse had expressed concerning the gaining of plenary indulgences by those in venial sin.[6a] It seems unobjectionable and as good as may be found.

Partial indulgences are usually qualified by the specification of the number of days or years; e. g. an indulgence of seven years, an indulgence of 300 days. Such expressions of time do not refer to the number of days or years by which one's confinement in Purgatory is shortened. But they signify that so much remission is granted by the indulgence as would have been obtained by a corresponding number of days or years spent in penance during the era of public penitential discipline. Now, in the ages of canonical penances the discipline was especially rigorous during the forty days of Lent, and, by the same token, the Lenten penance was especially expiatory. It is this circumstance that the Church has in mind when she grants indulgences of a certain number of quarantines; e. g. "an indulgence of seven years and seven quarantines." This is to be interpreted as the equivalent of the remission that would have accrued from spending seven years, exclusive of Lent, in ordinary penance under the ancient rule, and in addition to that, the remission gained by submitting to the much more rigorous and expiatory penance of seven Lenten seasons.[7]

There is now no limitation of the number of times that a partial indulgence may be gained, unless the brief of concession mentions such a limitation; "Unless the contrary is expressly stated, a partial indulgence may be gained often each day, if the prescribed work is repeated.'"[8]

B. Regarding their subject, indulgences may be either (a) general, or (b) particular, accordingly as they are granted in favor of all the faithful, or are restricted either to certain persons or to definite classes of persons. With reference to their subject, too, a distinction is to be made between indulgences (1) for the living, (2) for the dead, and (3) those for both the living and the dead. After the explanation of these terms given in the preceding chapter, little need be added here, except the legislation of Canon 930, to the effect that (excepting manifestly inalienable indulgences, of which more presently) all those granted by the Sovereign Pontiff are applicable to the dead. Vermeersch is of the opinion that Canon 930 is retroactive, so that all indulgences granted by the Popes of the past may now be applied to faithful departed.[9] A decree of the Congregation of Indulgences, September 15, 1852, declared that all indulgences contained in the official collection, the Raccolta are applicable to the Poor Souls.[10] Indulgences exclusively for the living are, by law, all those granted by inferiors of the Pope,[11] as are also, by their very nature, the indulgences granted for the moment of death.[11a] A well known example of an indulgence applicable to the dead alone is that granted by Pius X for each visit made to a church, public or semi-public oratory on All Souls' Day.[11b]

C. By reason of their duration, indulgences are: (a) perpetual, or (b) temporary. The former are granted without limitation as to time, under some such form as "ad perpetuam rei memoriam." The latter, on the other hand may be gained only within a specified period. Practically all indulgences are perpetual. And since indulgences are favors and receive a favorable interpretation,[12] all are to be presumed perpetual, unless the contrary is made clear. The only temporary indulgence of note is the Jubilee Indulgence, enduring for the space of a year.

D. Finally, by reason of the manner in which they are to be gained, indulgences are: (a) personal, (b) real, (c) local.

(a) Personal indulgences are those granted to physical persons, or to moral persons, such as pious associations, religious communities, etc. In reference to the indulgences granted to the members of pious associations, it is of interest to note that one may gain all the indulgences granted to the sodality or confraternity, even though one has been negligent in observing the statutes and regulations of the organization, provided only that the association has been canonically erected and the respective sodalist has been legitimately affiliated and fulfills all the conditions for gaining the indulgence.[12a] For the Congregation of Indulgences on January 25, 1842, declared: "The partial or general non-observance of statutes is no obstacle to the gaining of indulgences, for the reason that statutes are rather for the government and right administration of the sodality, and are not at all conditions or works enjoined for the gaining of indulgences."[13]

(b) Real indulgences are those attached to some portable thing, such as a Rosary or a medal.[14] Regarding real indulgences, a decision of the Congregation of Indulgences given on February 29, 1820, contains two points of special interest. The first of these is to the effect that one and the same object can be enriched with a number of indulgences.[15] And the Code substantially incorporates this decree, at the same time extending it to local indulgences: "Several indulgences under various titles can be attached to one and the same thing or place."[16] The second noteworthy point in the decision of 1820 is that indulgences can be attached only to objects that are not fragile. This same restriction is usually made with reference to the objects to which the Apostolic Indulgence is attached. Thus, the official list of Apostolic Indulgences for the current pontificate contains the following statement: "Things suitable for receiving the blessing for gaining the Apostolic Indulgences are only chaplets, etc., which are not made of tin, lead, glass, or other similar material, which is easily broken or worn out."[18] Hollow glass beads are unsuitable material, though solid glass objects may be enriched with indulgences.[18a] Ivory,[18b] iron, steel, marble, alabaster, and coral are also classed as suitable materials. Crosses and Crucifixes of wood may be indulgenced, though the figure of our Lord on the Crucifix must be of hard wood.[18c] To be enriched with indulgences, pictures and images may not be of paper, pasteboard, or linen.[18d] In the list of indulgences of Pius XI it is demanded that medals, statues, etc., to be fit objects for the Apostolic Indulgences must bear the images of Saints who have been duly canonized or who are included in approved martyrologies.[19] It is to be noted, however, that only one side of the medal need necessarily bear the image of a canonized Saint. The reverse may have an image of a Pope, the representation of a church, or other appropriate figures.[19a]

(c) Local indulgences, as defined by Fanfani: "Are those which are immediately attached to a pious place (as a church or chapel), or to a thing set up in a determined place (such as an altar, an image of a Saint)."[20] That local indulgences should extend to places, such as churches and chapels, is included in the meaning of the word, and therefore obvious. But the extension of "local" to the altars in a church may seem far-fetched, since we are wont to regard altars as things, not as places. However, the extension of the term in the present instance is justified by analogy with the Code, which enumerates altars among the "loca sacra."[21] The further extension of the word "local" to images and statues reserved in the church is vouched for by the majority of authors, so far at least as the present matter is concerned. The reasonableness of calling images and statues "places" appears from the circumstance that rescripts attaching an indulgence to an image or a statue in a church invariably grant the indulgence to those who "visit" the statue; and the objective of a visit is a place, not a thing. There is no warrant, however, for applying "local" to the indulgences granted by prelates in the places subject to their jurisdiction, as has been done by one very recent author: "These indulgences are called local because they apply only to the territory over which a prelate has jurisdiction."[22]

NOTES ON CHAPTER IV.

1 Decr. Auth. S. C. Indul. et Reliq., 356.

2 Canon 921, 3.

3 Canon 928, 1.

3a St. Alphonsus, Theologia Moralis, VI, 534; Fanfani, de Indulgentiis, 10.

4 Vermeersch, "Epitome Juris Canonici," 11, 201, 1; St. Alphonsus, Theol. Mor., VI, 534.

5 Canon 926.

6 Vermeersch, "Epitome Juris Canonici," II, 201, 6.

6a St. Alphonsus, Theol. Mor., VI, 534.

7 Paulus, "Geschichte des Ablasses im Mittelalter," II, 73.

8 Canon 928, 1; Acta Ap. Sedis, VI, 379.

9 Vermeersch, "Epitome Juris Canonici," II, 201, 6.

10 Decr. Auth. S. C. Indul. et Reliq., 361.

11 Canon 912, 2.

11a Canon 468, 2.

11b Acta Ap. Sedis, VI, 378.

12 Vermeersch, "Epitome Juris Canonici," II, 206.

12a Fanfani, "De Indulgentiis," 42.
13 Decr. Auth. S. C. Indul. et Reliq., 298.
14 Fanfani, "De Indulgentiis," 9.
15 Decr. Auth. S. C. Indul. et Reliq., 249, 3. "An uni et eidem rei, puta uni coronae, possint applicari plures indulgentiae, v. g. indulgentiae dictae Apostolicae, et indulgentiae dictae S. Birgittae? Resp Affirmative, dummodo ad eas lucrandas renoventur opera injuncta iterabilia."
16 Canon 933.
17 Decr. Auth. S. C. Indul. et Reliq., 249, 2; Decr. Auth. S. C. Indul. et Reliq., 333.
18 Acta Ap. Sedis, XV, 143.
18a Decr. Auth. S. C. Indul. et Reliq., 249, 1-2.
18b Decr. Auth. S. C. Indul. et Reliq., 271, 2.
18c Beringer-Steinen, "Die Ablaesse," I, 401.
18d Beringer-Steinen, "Die Ablaesse," I, 401.
19 Act Ap. Sedis, XV, 143.
19a Decr. Auth. S. C. Indul. et Reliq., 32; Beringer-Steinen, "Die Ablaesse," I, 402.
20 Fanfani, "De Indulgentiis," 9.
21 Cf. Lib. III, Pars. II, Tit. II.
22 Augustine, "The Pastor," 104.

CHAPTER V.

COMPETENCE TO GRANT INDULGENCES.

Indulgences, being a participation in the common treasury of the Church, are properly within the disposal of the authority to whom that treasure has been committed in trust. The Pope alone, as the Vicar of Jesus Christ, has the primary and supreme power over the concession of indulgences. "In its fulness the power of granting indulgences resides in the Pope, who can concede them as he wills, provided there exists a legitimate cause."[1] The same doctrine is expressed in the Code: "Besides the Roman Pontiff, to whom the disposal of the entire spiritual treasury of the Church has been committed by Christ the Lord, etc."[2] And certainly, if the exposition made in the second chapter,—concerning the existence in the Church of the power to grant indulgences—means anything, then the fulness of that power must reside in the supreme possessor of ecclesiastical authority.

Besides the Holy Father, the successors of the Apostles in the Roman Catholic episcopate also participate in this power, and that in virtue of their office (potestas ordinaria), but always subject to the restrictions imposed by the supreme authority. Thus much may be gathered from the twenty-eighth question proposed to the Wicliffites and Hussites in the Bull "Inter Cunctos" of Martin V: "Whether he believes that single Bishops can grant such indulgences to their subjects, according to the limitation of the sacred canons."[3] Likewise St. Thomas: "But in Bishops (this power of granting indulgences) is limited according to the ordinance of the Pope, and therefore they can do as much as is ordained, and no more.'"[4] Similarly Canon 912 says: "Besides the Roman Pontiff—only those can grant indulgences by ordinary power to whom it is expressly conceded by law."[5]

In the law several classes of persons are enumerated who enjoy the power of granting indulgences. The first mentioned in the Code are Cardinals. By law, Cardinals are empowered to grant indulgences of 200 days.[6] Such indulgences may be gained toties quoties by persons and in places subject to the Cardinals' jurisdiction or under their patronage, but may be gained only once, and that by persons actually present at the place of concession, if the Cardinal grants an indulgence in a place outside his jurisdiction. To illustrate: a Cardinal in the church assigned to him as titular may attach an indulgence of 200 days to visiting a certain statue, and that indulgence may be gained as often as the visit is made. But if he were to attach an indulgence to a statue in some other part of the world, the indulgence could be gained but once. Metropolitans have the power of granting an indulgence of 100 days in their own sees as well as in their suffragen sees.[7] Residential Bishops[8] and Prefects and Vicars Apostolic[9] (even though the latter lack the episcopal character) may grant indulgences of 50 days within the territory subject to them. Other than these, no one in the Church possesses the ordinary power of granting indulgences.

In ages past, less restriction was placed on the exercise of this power by prelates inferior to the Pope. It appears that an imprudent generosity amounting in some instances to prodigality, occasioned not a little abuse and scandal. To eliminate this, Pope Innocent III at the Fourth Lateran Council decided to limit the concessions of inferior prelates. To this end he decreed that indulgences granted on the occasion of the dedication of a church should not exceed one year for the day of dedication and forty days for the anniversary, regardless of who the consecrator was. The same decree sets forty days as the limit of all other indulgences granted by any inferior of the Pope.[10] However, certain theologians taught that Archbishops could grant indulgences of 80 days, and as a matter of fact a custom was established in South America whereby Archbishops of that country granted indulgences of 80 days.[10a] By a rescript of the Congregation of Extraordinary Ecclesiastical Affairs, issued in 1899, Leo XIII approved the custom of the South American Archbishops.[10b] On August 28, 1903, Pius X conceded that in future Cardinals might grant indulgences of 200 days, Archbishops of 100 days, and Bishops of 50 days.[10c] This legislation of Pius X has been incorporated in the Code.

In Canon 913 are contained other restrictions with which the law hedges in the ordinary power conceded to the prelates enumerated in the preceding paragraphs. That Canon reads: "Inferiors of the Roman Pontiff cannot I. Grant to others the faculty of conceding indulgences, unless they have received an express indult to that effect from the Holy See; II. Concede indulgences applicable to the departed; III. Attach to a thing or a pious act or a sodality to which indulgences have already been attached by the Apostolic See or by some one else, new indulgences, unless new conditions are prescribed."

The first paragraph of Canon 913 gives occasion to introduce the question of delegated jurisdiction in the matter of indulgences. One would suppose that, being part of the ordinary power, the power to grant indulgences could be delegated. Melata is authority for the statement that authors commonly taught that one who had ordinary power to grant indulgences could also delegate the power to others, but he adds the observation: "Nevertheless it seems less becoming that inferiors of the Pope should use this faculty."[11] The Code definitely settles the matter. It is true that Canon 199,1 stipulates that whoever has ordinary jurisdiction can delegate it in whole or in part. But the proviso is added: "Unless it is expressly provided otherwise by the law." And Canon 913,1 expressly forbids the delegation of the ordinary power to grant indulgences.

It goes without saying that the Pope can delegate his jurisdiction in this sphere to others. But not all the faithful are apt subjects of such delegation. Here Canon 118 has application, prescribing that only clerics are capable of ecclesiastical jurisdiction. And since the granting of indulgences entails jurisdiction, only clerics may be delegated to this charge. However, it is not required that the cleric be a prelate, a priest, or that he even be in orders. For the concession of indulgences does not involve sacramental administration.[13] Therefore, strictly speaking, there is nothing to prohibit a tonsured cleric from being delegated by the Supreme Pontiff to grant indulgences. Incidentally, faculties are granted to Ordinaries in missionary countries to grant indulgences far in excess of the concessions which even Cardinals may make. And, what is more, the same faculties empower the Ordinaries of missionary places to subdelegate this jurisdiction in nearly every case where such subdelegation could serve a practical purpose.[14]

Little need said in explanation of the second paragraph of Cannon 913, withholding from prelates the right to concede indulgences applicable to the departed souls. It is not from intrinsic reasons that such a prohibition has been made. There is nothing repugnant in the act whereby the Pope's inferior would grant an indulgence so applicable. A very recent proof of this assertion is at hand in the formula of faculties granted to the Ordinaries in missionary countries, to which reference has just been made. The twentieth concession enumerated in that list reads: "The faculty of conceding that all the above-named indulgences may be applied to the souls detained in Purgatory."[14] Additional importance attaches to this faculty insofar as it shows that, although Canon 913,2 makes no mention of the fact, still the Pope may delegate a Cardinal, Archbishop, or Bishop to make applicable to the souls in Purgatory the indulgences which they grant in virtue of their ordinary power, as well as all those indulgences for the granting of which a delegated jurisdiction has been received. Vermeersch observes that the prohibition of prelates inferior to the Pope from granting indulgences applicable to the dead was not certain until the promulgation of the Code. And he voices the opinion that, if in the past some prelates granted indulgences for the departed, they are not revoked.[15] His opinion is apparently correct. Nothing compels us to assume that indulgences of whatever kind, once validly granted by prelates in the exercise of ordinary or delegated jurisdiction, have been recalled by the Code.

A final restriction imposed on prelates is contained in the third paragraph of Canon 913. It deals with the cumulation of indulgences, due to successive concessions of different prelates. As early as December 17, 1838, the Congregation of Indulgences issued a decisions repudiating such cumulation. A certain citizen of Marseilles owned a statue of the Blessed Virgin to which the local Bishop had attached an indulgence of forty days. The over-zealous citizen was in the habit of asking every Bishop who chanced to pass through the city to add an indulgence of forty days to the same statue. A doubt proposed to the Sacred Congregation was answered to the effect that only the first indulgence, that granted by the local Bishop, was valid.[16]

Canon 913,3 presents the full development of the Church's intention to eliminate superfluous, indiscreetly granted indulgences. Herein it is forbidden, first of all, to add a new indulgence to an object previously enriched by papal indulgences. Inferiors of the Pope can therefore make no increase in the indulgences which he has attached, for instance, to objects of the Apostolic Indulgence (re), or to the Way of the Cross (actui pietatis), or to the Priests' Eucharistic League (sodalitio). Moreover, once an object, an exercise, or a sodality has been indulgenced by another prelate, be he a contemporary in the Church, a predecessor in office, or any other, thereafter no prelate may increase the indulgence, not even with the consent of the first prelate.[17] There is here a sort of pre-emption by which the first to grant an indulgence, by that very act excludes all prelates inferior to the Pope from indulgencing the same object. This pre-emption, it need scarcely be said, cannot be invoked against the Pope. His supreme power to grant indulgences to objects of piety remains unaffected, regardless of the favors which others have attached to these objects. Moreover, the concluding words of Canon 913,3: "Unless new conditions are prescribed," restrict the prohibition. The prohibition does not exist whenever the second prelate adds a new condition not mentioned by the first. Thus, if the Bishop grants an indulgence of fifty days to all who visit an altar in the cathedral church, nothing prevents his successor in office from granting an additional fifty days for visiting the same altar during the celebration of Mass thereat. However, this does not enable one prelate to divide an object or a pious exercise previously indulgenced by another, and to apply a separate indulgence to each of the component parts. To illustrate: since the Way of the Cross has been favored with indulgences by the Pope, a Cardinal could not grant a separate and distinct indulgence for making the first, tenth, and fourteenth Stations, for example, in his titular church.[18]

The statement has been made that the Holy Father is the supreme dispenser of indulgences. But he does not, as a rule, discharge this function personally. It has long been committed to the care of a specially designated section of the Roman Curia. In the course of history, the discharge of affairs appertaining to indulgences has several times been changed from one Congregation to another. Pope Clement VIII, noting that the indulgence legislation of the Fourth Lateran and the Tridentine Councils was not being observed, instituted a special commission of Cardinals to attend to the enforcement of the conciliar decrees. In a few decades, however, this commission ceased, and matters of indulgence fell to the competence of the Congregations of the Inquisition and of the Council.[18a] On August 4, 1667, Clement IX began the organization of the Congregation of Indulgences and Relics.[19] By the Constitution "In Ipsis Pontificatus Nostri Primordiis," dated July 10, 1669, the Pope defined the scope of this Congregation and erected it permanently.[20] The Congregation thus erected continued until 1904 to superintend whatever pertained to indulgences. However, all questions involving the dogmatic aspects of indulgences were excepted from the competence of this Congregation. These matters of dogma were reserved to the Holy Office. In 1904 Pius X united the Congregation of Indulgences with the Congregation of Rites, the former, however, retaining its specific duties and powers, to be exercised under the Prefect of the Congregation of Rites.[20a] Another change was made in 1908. In the reorganization of the Curia, which Pius X effected by the Constitution "Sapienti Consilio," the Congregation of Indulgences and Relics was dissolved. The Constitution transferred to the Holy Office all matters involving indulgences, which matters were to be attended to by a special committee known as the "Sectio de Indulgentiis." Finally, the Code commits to the Tribunal of the Sacred Penitentiary that complex of questions involved in indulgences which between 1669 and 1908 had been the peculiar province of the Congregation of Indulgences and Relics, questions of dogma still remaining subject to the Holy Office.[21] In formally conceding indulgences, the Sacred Tribunal either issues a simple rescript, or it commits to the Secretary of Briefs the charge of expediting a brief containing the concession of the indulgence.[22]

To avoid possibilities of abuse, it has been the purpose of the Church to give exclusive control over indulgences to the Congregation entrusted with them. So true is this that any general concession of indulgences must be brought to the Congregation's attention, under pain of nullity. Accordingly, a decree of the Congregation of Indulgences states: "Since daily experience shows that many general concessions of indulgences are made without the knowledge of this Congregation, and since from this practice arise many abuses and much confusion, by the present decree the Congregation declares that hereafter those who obtain such general concessions must, under penalty of forfeiting the favor obtained, present to the secretary of this Sacred Congregation an exemplar of such concessions."[23] In Canon 920 this decree is made a general law, the term "general concessions" being replaced by the more explanatory phrase "Concessions by the Supreme Pontiff for all the faithful." Therefore, should the Holy Father grant, either viva voce or by private letter, any indulgence in which all the faithful share, that concession is null and void unless the authentic exemplar is forwarded to the Sacred Penitentiary. And by the exemplar is understood the original written document signed by the Pope, if the concession was in writing; or in case of an oral concession, a written document over the signature of an official whose testimony to the fact of the oral concession is acceptable. Vermeersch interprets the phrase "for all the faithful" of Canon 920 strictly, limiting it to those indulgences which all the faithful may gain anywhere and at any time, without the use of a blessed object, and he excludes those indulgences for which a visit to some church is prescribed.[24]

Very intimately associated with the concession of indulgences is the so-called communication of them. The difference between the two consists in this, that by communication no new indulgence is granted, but one previously granted by competent authority is through the so-called communication of privileges extended to subjects not embraced by the original concession. An indulgence is said to be communicated when, after having been granted to one class of persons, it becomes accessible to another class. For instance: if to an arch-confraternity is granted a plenary indulgence with the privilege of communicating it to the confraternities which aggregate themselves with the arch-confraternity, then as soon as a confraternity becomes legitimately aggregated its members have access to the indulgence, without further intervention on the part of religious or other authorities. All communication of indulgences, to be valid, must be approved by the granter of the original indulgence.[24a] Furthermore, the formalities prescribed for the act of aggregation must be exactly observed. What these formalities are will differ in different organizations. Hence the document of concession of the indulgence and the constitutions of the society must be consulted in individual cases.

NOTES ON CHAPTER V.

1 Summa Theologica, Suppl. q. 26, art. 3.
2 Canon 912.
3 Denzinger-Bannwart, "Enchiridion," 678.
4 Summa Theologica, Suppl. q. 26, art. 3.
5 Canon 912.
6 Canon 239, i, 24.
7 Canon 274, 2.
8 Canon 349, ii, 2.
9 Canon 294, 2.
10 C. 12, X, de excessibus praelatorum et subditorum, V, 31.
10a Beringer-Steinen, "Die Ablaesse," I, 47.
10b Acta Sanctae Sedis, XXXI, 758.
10c Acta Sanctae Sedis, XXXVI, 318.
11 Melata, "Manuale de Indulgentiis," I, iii, 2, 2.
12 Quodlibeta, II, xvi, ad 2.
13 Vermeersch, "De Formulis Facultatum S. C. de Prop. Fide Commentaria," 63-74.
14 Vermeersch, "De Formulis Facultatum S. C. de Prop. Fide Commentaria," 70.
15 Vermeersch, "Epitome Juris Canonici," II, 203.
16 Decr. Auth. S. C. Indul. et Reliq., 265.
17 Decr. Auth. S. C. Indul. et Reliq., 433, 1-2.
18 Decr. Auth. S. C. Indul. et Reliq., 433, 5.
18a Beringer-Steinen, "Die Ablaesse," I, 144.
19 Decr. Auth. S. C. Indul. et Reliq., VIII, note.
20 Decr. Auth. S. C. Indul. et Reliq., VI.
20a Beringer-Steinen, "Die Ablaesse," I, 148.
21 Canon 258, 2.
22 Vermeersch, "Epitome Juris Canonici," II, 205.
23 Decr. Auth. S. C. Indul. et Reliq., 205.
24 Vermeersch, "Epitome Juris Canonici," II, 105.
24a Fanfani, "De Indulgentiis," 18.

CHAPTER VI.

Subjects Capable of Gaining Indulgences.

The dogma of indulgences, as has been said, is a corollary of the principle of vicarious satisfaction, the doctrine of the treasure of the Church, and that of the Communion of Saints. Christ shed His Blood for the Redemption of all mankind. And there is laid up a wealth of satisfactions sufficient to atone for all the debts which the children of Adam have contracted before the Divine Justice. Yet, just as there are some who will place themselves beyond the pale of Christ's Redemption, so too, there are many for whom the riches of satisfaction stored away in the Church will prove to be no boon. From the fact that a treasure of indulgences exists it does not follow that indulgences are to be broadcasted indiscriminately as pearls cast before swine. The Church, is, indeed, by divine appointment the dispenser of the accumulated satisfactions of Christ and the Saints. But at the same time she is the custodian of them, commissioned to communicate them only to those whom proper credentials identify as apt subjects of indulgences.

The first mark admitting one to the depository of the Church is the sacred seal of Baptism. "In order that one be capable of gaining indulgences for himself, he must be baptized."[1] In Baptism it is that we "put on Christ." Baptism it is which enrolls us in that select society, the Communion of Saints, to whose membership is restricted the circulation of that currency whose every coin bears the image of Christ and the inscription "Indulgence." An alien does not share in the bounty of a nation. Likewise an alien to the kingdom of Christ, one not naturalized, not re-born into the Church through Baptism, does not participate in the peculiar bounty which the Church has in her power to bestow. "By Baptism man is constituted a person in the Church of Christ with all the rights and offices of Christians."[1a] Accordingly, the pagan and the infidel, even the well-disposed catechumen are not considered subjects of indulgences.

Once a member of the Church, always a member, is axiomatic. The character of Baptism is indelible. Therefore one cannot cease to be a Christian, one cannot evade the responsibilities which being a Catholic entails; one cannot lay aside the yoke of Christ and dispense oneself from the burdens, the obligations, the laws imposed by the Church. But indulgences are not a burden. They are a privilege and a benefit. And as such, they may be withheld from those whom the Church judges unworthy of them.[1b] Those who are recalcitrant, who withdraw themselves, so far as they are able, from the communion of the Church, may with propriety be excluded from her favors and privileges until they abandon their waywardness. Therefore the excommunicated—whether they be "excommunicati vitandi" or "excommunicati tolerati"—cannot gain indulgences until the bann of excommunication is lifted: "In order that one be capable of gaining indulgences for himself, he must be—not excommunicated."[2] And: "Whoever is excommunicated does not become a participant in the indulgences, etc."[3]

But what of the multitude of Christians who, through no fault of their own, are outside the pale of the Church; the heretics and the schismatics who are in good faith? These are not totally separated from the Church, for, as theologians express it, they remain united with the soul of the Church. While it is true that the Church has enacted no explicit law barring them from indulgences, nevertheless they seem to be ineligible. They belong to the soul of the Church, forsooth, but they are cut off from visible communion with her, they are separated from the body of the Church, they are not members of the visible society. And it is as a visible society that the Church dispenses indulgences; it is with her external jurisdiction that the supervision of indulgences is bound up. Her voluntary jurisdiction the Church exercises over those who are members of her as a corporate society. To partake of the benefit of indulgences, one must be in a position to partake of those goods which come from the Church as from a corporate society, one must be within the corporate union of the Church. And being in no such position of vantage, heretics and schismatics are not subjects of indulgence.[4]

The passing reference in the preceding paragraph to the fact that indulgences are dependent on the Church's external jurisdiction indicates that not every member of the Church, even in good standing, is by that fact alone eligible to all the indulgences that are granted. Jurisdiction in the matter of indulgences is exercised by a number of superiors, each of whom, save one, moves within a limited sphere. Now: "The power of jurisdiction can be directly exercised only over subjects."[5] The various ecclesiastical superiors inferior to the Roman Pontiff can directly grant indulgences only to their immediate subjects. Strictly speaking, therefore, it follows that only subjects of the respective superior may avail themselves of indulgences that have been granted. To this end Canon 925,1 enacts: "In order that one be capable of gaining indulgences for himself, he must be a subject of the granter." This legislation had been anticipated by the Congregation of Indulgences in answering the question: "Whether indulgences which the Bishop grants are valid only within the limits of his diocese, or also outside the diocese?" To this the Congregation answered: "Affirmative to the first part; negative to the second part, unless there be question of subjects of the Bishop, or question of personal indulgences."[6] That is to say, indulgences granted by a Bishop may be gained only within the territory of the Bishop; but subjects of the Bishop may gain the indulgences anywhere, and if the indulgences are personal they may be gained by anyone at any place.

Indulgences are favors granted by the Church, and that their privileged character might appear to advantage, the Church modifies the expression "subject of the granter." There is no modification in the part of the decree of the Congregation of Indulgences just quoted, wherein subjects of the Bishop may gain indulgences granted by him, even though they are outside his territory.[7] A modification was introduced in the same decision when the Congregation declared that indulgences granted by the Bishop could be gained by non-subjects sojourning within the diocesan limits, provided these indulgences had not been granted to a peculiar community of persons, such as a religious community.[8] A modification similar to the foregoing has been incorporated into the Code, which declares that subjects while outside the diocese, visitors to the diocese with a domicile elsewhere, and those in the diocese who have no domicile whatever, as well as exempt religious sojourning in the diocese may gain indulgences granted by the Bishop, unless the terms of the concession determine otherwise.[9] To sum up: although as a rule a superior can concede indulgences only to subjects resident within the limits of his jurisdiction, once those indulgences have been granted, and provided the document of concession contained no stipulation to the contrary, they may be gained even by "peregrini" and "vagi" who happen into the diocese. Also, unless otherwise provided, indulgences granted by a superior may be gained by his subjects, no matter where they are. By Canon 927, even those religious who are exempt from the jurisdiction of Ordinaries, become subjects to the extent of being able to avail themselves of the indulgences granted by the Bishop of the territory in which they are. The exceptional case provided in Canon 1166,3, by which any prelate dedicating a church, even outside his own territory, may grant an indulgence, has been treated in the preceding chapter when dealing with the question of authorities who may grant indulgences.

The question may be raised: To what extent are Catholics of Oriental rites subject to Western jurisdiction in the matter of indulgences? Canon 1, exempting Oriental Catholics from the legislation of the Code, apparently gave rise to the doubt in the minds of some Eastern prelates as to whether Oriental Catholics were capable of gaining the indulgences current in the Western Church. Their doubt was proposed to the Sacred Penitentiary: "Whether the faithful of the Oriental Rites can gain all indulgences granted by the Supreme Pontiff in a universal decree?" The Sacred Tribunal answered: "Affirmative. And this response His Holiness, Pope Benedict XV—ordered to become public law."[10]

The state of sanctifying grace is necessary to constitute one a subject of indulgences to be gained for oneself. In the words of Canon 925: "In order that one be capable of gaining indulgences for himself, he must be in the state of grace." St. Thomas sets forth the reason on which such a law is based as follows: "A dead member does not receive any influence from living members; but he who is in the state of mortal sin, is, so to speak, a dead member; therefore he receives no influence from the merits of living members by way of indulgences.'"[11] A further reason arises from the fact that the temporal punishment due to sin cannot be remitted while the eternal punishment remains uncancelled.[11a]

The state of grace is demanded at the time the indulgence is to be imparted. Accordingly, when a series of good works is made the condition of gaining an indulgence, it is only when the last work of the series is being performed that the state of grace must be realized, for it is at the moment of completion of the final work of the series that the indulgence is actually imparted.[12] Thus Benedict XIV in legislating for the Jubilee of 1750 writes: "Although we are ever more and more desirous that the visiting of the churches be done in the state of grace,—We think that those are not at all to be excluded from the fruit of the indulgences who, without previous confession, begin and continue the visits to the churches, provided only that when they complete the last work, in which the indulgence is acquired, they are in the state of grace"[13] So, too, the Code says: "In order that, etc.—he must be in the state of grace at least at the end of the prescribed works."[14] If, therefore, one begins the series of works in the state of mortal sin, or if, having begun in the state of grace, one falls into grievous sin in the course of the exercises, the letter of the law does not obilge one, under pain of forfeiting the indulgence, to regain sanctifying grace until the final work of the series has been reached.

There is in the law no specification of the means to be employed in putting oneself in the state of grace. Confession, the usual means, is not demanded. Therefore an act of perfect contrition is sufficient. This is the conclusion at which Beringer [15] arrives, in discussing the case where one, having made the Confession prescribed as one of the conditions or works necessary for gaining the indulgence, relapses into mortal sin before reaching the conclusion of the series of prescribed works. The Confession need not be repeated, he says, but an act of perfect contrition will serve the purpose of acquiring the sanctifynig grace demanded for the gaining of the indulgence. The same author notes no opposition to his opinion in the decision of the Congregation of Indulgences, which answered "Affirmative," to the proposed doubt: "Whether in the ordinary and extraordinary Jubilee all the rules of Benedict XIV are to be observed, which are not contrary to the Jubilee Bull?"[16] And the rules laid down by Benedict XIV included the following: "If after Confession and before completing all the works prescribed for gaining this Jubilee, one falls into mortal sin, the Confession must be repeated before completing the last of the other prescribed works, in order to gain the indulgence granted in this Jubilee."[17] This legislation demanding Confession as a means of acquiring grace binds only in the case of the Jubilee indulgence.[17a] However, the circumstance that Benedict XIV demanded another Confession for the gaining of the Jubilee Indulgence, and the fact that the Church is wont to make Confession one of the conditions for gaining a plenary indulgence, point to a desire, though by no means a command, that Confession, and not merely an act of contrition, be the means employed for arriving at the state of grace required for the gaining of an indulgence.[18]

While it is beyond dispute that the state of grace is demanded for gaining indulgences for oneself, an interminable controversy rages about the possibility of gaining indulgences for the departed while one is in the state of mortal sin. Asked a decisive solution of the question on two occasions, the Congregation of Indulgences refrained. On August 20, 1822, it answered the question: "Whether to gain the indulgences directly or indirectly granted for the dead, the state of grace is necessarily required?" The answer was: "Dilata."[19] And on February 22, 1847, the same question was answered: "Consult the approved authors."[20] An authoritative decision has not been rendered up to the present time, nor has the question been settled by the Code. For Canon 925,1 does not touch the requirement of the state of grace for gaining indulgences for the Poor Souls, insofar as it only prescribes: "In order that one be capable of gaining indulgences *for himself* (Ut quis sibi, etc.) he must be in the state of grace."[21] "Sibi" shows that the stipulation of Canon 925 refers with certainty only to the indulgences which the faithful wish to apply to themselves, not to those which they desire to offer in suffrage for the souls in Purgatory.

One is constrained, therefore, to consult the approved authors. And the consultation will bring one little nearer the solution than one is at the outset. For authors of the highest repute range themselves on either side in the controversy.

Among those who demand the state of grace as necessary for gaining indulgences for the dead is Palmieri, whose argument is: "Since he who applies to the departed the indulgence which he gains acts as a suffragan, we rightly demand in him that condition which is demanded in those who would offer satisfactions for others; namely, the state of divine friendship."[22] St. Alphonsus [23] and De Lugo [24] advocate the same opinion, the former characterizing it as "verior." The principle on which these theologians base their contention is that no one can apply to another what he has not acquired himself; but without sanctifying grace one cannot acquire indulgences for oneself; therefore one cannot apply them to the souls in Purgatory.

The contrary opinion is championed by such authors as Suarez,[25] Bellarmine,[26] and more recently, by Sabetti-Barrett,[27] who calls it "probabilior," though in another place he concedes: "The first opinion is to be urged practically, since it is safer."[28] The general argument advanced by this class of authors is that the Pope immediately and directly concedes the indulgence to the dead, requiring of the living only as a necessary condition the performance of certain objectively good works, which may be performed in the state of mortal sin. The worth of the satisfactions depends, not on the work performed, but on the concession of the Church. Again, as Beringer states it: "The sin of him who fulfills the enjoined conditions is no hindrance to the indulgences being applied to these pure souls, since these, just because they are innocent, are also capable of participating in the satisfactions of Christ and the Saints."[29]

To render a final decision in the controversy is for a more competent judge. It would seem that the argument put forth by those affirming the necessity of grace, namely, the argument that one cannot apply an indulgence to another until one has gained it for oneself, begs the question. Everyone admits that the sinner cannot gain an indulgence for himself while in mortal sin. But that has no place in the controversy. The point at issue is whether the sinner must really make the indulgence his, and then apply it to the suffering souls, or whether the Church applies it directly to the latter. And that issue the argument under discussion evades. Also the argument employed by Palmieri[30] is open to exception. It, too, states that the sinner must gain the indulgence for himself, and then apply it; the very thing to be proved. Moreover, Palmieri, aware that indulgences are to be applied to the Poor Souls only by way of suffrage, takes for granted that the person performing the works must be the suffragan. He disregards the fact that the Church, through her visible head, is better qualified in every way than any private individual to offer to God some of her satisfactions in suffrage for the suffering souls: in other words, the Church, and not the person who performs the prescribed works, is the suffragan for the souls in Purgatory.[31]

On the whole, the presentation of their case by the authors cited above (De Lugo, St. Alphonsus, Palmieri) reveals a noticeable absence of convincing argument supporting the contention that the state of grace is indispensable for gaining indulgences for the Poor Souls. And in the absence of such proof one is inclined to favor the opposite opinion.

An objection may be formulated from the circumstance that in gaining indulgences the conditions of Confession and Communion or at least a contrite heart are required as necessary works, no matter to whom the indulgence is to be applied.[32] And since these conditions connote the state of grace, it follows that the state of grace is necessary to gain any indulgence whatever. It may be answered that by a decision of the Congregation of Indulgences the formula "corde saltem contrito" is never a condition or a part of the work enjoined, but that, whenever prescribed, it is merely a disposition.[33] As to Confession and Communion, a distinction has to be introduced. If Confession and Communion are the sole conditions for gaining the indulgence, then there is no escape from the conclusion that gaining that particular indulgence for the Poor Souls demands the state of grace. For these Sacraments must be received worthily, in such a manner as to confer grace on the soul. But from the standpoint of indulgence, this state of grace is something accidental; it is a requirement of the nature of Confession and Communion; it is not a requirement of the gaining of indulgences for the dead. And for this reason, if besides these Sacraments some third condition, e. g., an alms, be enjoined, then the ordering of the three exercises can be so arranged that the state of grace is not necessarily a concomitant of the indulgence. This would be verified if Confession, Communion, and a lapse into mortal sin preceded the giving of the alms. For then the grace necessarily resulting from the Sacraments would no longer be present in the soul when the indulgence accrued, that is, on the completion of the alms deed. Therefore the objection is not valid that to gain an indulgence for the dead the state of sanctifying grace is required at least in those cases in which Confession, Communion, or perfect contrition are prescribed. The objection holds only when the above mentioned conditions are the sole requirements for gaining the indulgence; not if some third condition is added.

Two observations of practical piety, one in reference to each party of the disputants, may conclude these remarks on an old controversy. The first of these is that the milder opinion is not without great advantage, insofar as one who has had the misfortune of committing grave sin should not on that account refrain from at least endeavoring to gain indulgences for the Poor Souls. The mild opinion gives him well founded hope that his endeavors will actually succeed, and his charity to the sufferers in Purgatory will facilitate his own return to grace.[34] The other observation is that, whatever be the theoretical aspect of the dispute, Catholics should make their charity to the Poor Souls as certainly effective as in their power lies, by always remaining in a condition to aid the departed with more than mere probability.

Some intention is required to gain a indulgence. Canon 925,2 states the principle as follows: "In order that the subject who is capable really gain them (sc. indulgences), he must have at least the general intention of gaining them." Indulgences are benefits, and in the ordinary course of events, benefits are conferred only on those who in some way have the will to receive them. Again, the good works to which indulgences accrue, having a meritorious value attached to them, it would seem that some intention is necessary in order to realize the indulgence value of these works, over and above the meritorious value. A general intention is all that the Code demands for the gaining of an indulgence. A general intention is here distinguished from a specific intention. It may be described as the will to acquire whatever indulgences attach to the works one performs. One may have such a general intention without knowing what the indulgences in question are, or without even being aware that the work one is performing has been enriched with indulgences. The Catholic who makes the general intention of gaining all the indulgences he possibly can may, and in all likelihood will, perform works to which are attached indulgences whose very existence he did not know. His ignorance is no impediment to the gaining of the indulgences.

As to the character of the required intention, whether it must be actual, virtual, or habitual, a distinction is to be made between those indulgences which one desires to retain for oneself and those which one wishes to apply to the departed. Discussion of the latter may be left to the chapter dealing with the application of indulgences to others. To be gained for ourselves, indulgences require at least a habitual intention, that is, an act of the will once made and not revoked, though not actually influencing our present action.[35] This statement may seem to contradict the assertion of some authors, to the effect that a virtual intention is necessary. The discrepancy, however, is due solely to a difference in terminology, these latter authors employing the term "virtual" to express what others usually include under the adjective "habitual."[36] Beringer illustrates the efficacy of the habitual intention as follows: "That one no longer thinks of that intention, that it exerts no appreciable influence on our present activity, even that one recites the one or other indulgenced prayer out of a different motive (provided that motive does not exclude the gaining of the indulgence) all this matters not; for that general habitual intention always endures, and that suffices."[37]

Without impugning the adequacy of the habitual intention, authors unanimously recommend a higher form of intention; and with reason. For it cannot but conduce to one's appreciation of indulgences and contribute notably to the zeal and devotion with which one performs the works prescribed for gaining them, if one keeps the gaining of the indulgence in mind by a virtual, or, better still, by an actual intention. So the theoretical extreme represented by those authors who declare that a habitual intention of sufficient intensity for gaining all indulgences is expressed by the bare purpose and resolve of leading a Christian life, is counterbalanced by the recommendation which most authors offer with Beringer,[38] quoting the Raccolta: "It would be very advisable to renew every morning the intention of gaining each day each and every one of the indulgences that can be gained during the day."[39]

NOTES ON CHAPTER VI.

1 Canon 925, 1.
1a Canon 87.
1b Canon 87.
2 Canon 925, 1.
3 Canon 2262, 1.
4 Fanfani, "De Indulgentiis," 28.
5 Canon 201, 1.
6 Collectanea S. C. P. F., 2003, ad 1.
7 Collectanea S. C. P. F., 2003, ad 1 et 3.
8 Collectanea S. C. P. F., 2003, ad 2.
9 Canon 927.
10 S. Poenitentiaria, 7 July, 1917, Acta Ap. Sedis, IX, 399.
11 Summa Theologica, Suppl. q. 27, art. 1.
11a St. Alphonsus, "Theologia Moralis," VI, 533.
12 Beringer-Hilgers, "Die Ablaesse," I, 112; Layman, "Theologia Moralis," V, vii, 5.
13 Benedict XIV, const. "Inter. Praeteritos," 76.
14 Canon 925, 1.
15 Beringer-Steinen, "Die Ablaesse," I, 86.
16 Decreta Auth. S. C. Indul. et Reliq., 353.
17 Benedict XIV, const. "Convocatis," XLVII.
17a Beringer-Steinen, "Die Ablaesse," I, 86.
18 Beringer-Hilgers, "Die Ablaesse," I, 113.
19 Decr. Auth. S. C. Indul. et Reliq., 353.
20 Decr. Auth. S. C. Indul. et Reliq., 341.
21 Canon 925, 1.
22 Tractatus de Poenitentia, Appendix de Indulgentiis, IV.
23 Theologia Moralis, VI, 534.
24 De Sacramento Poenitentiae, Disp. XXVII, sec. v, 75.
25 De Sacramento Poenitentiae, Disp. LIII, sec. iv.
26 De Indulgentiis et Jubilaeo Libri Duo, I, xiv.
27 Compendium Theologiae Moralis, 1049, ii, 3.
28 Compendium Theologiae Moralis, 1050, 9.
29 Beringer-Hilgers, "Die Ablaesse," I, 114.
30 Palmieri, Tractatus de Poenitentia," Appendix de Indulgentiis, IV.
31 Augustine, "Commentary on the New Canon Law, IV, 387.
32 Beringer-Hilgers, "Die Ablaesse," I, 114.
33 Decr. Auth. S. C. Indulg. et Reliq., 427.
34 Beringer-Hilgers, "Die Ablaesse," I, 114.
35 Pruemmer, "Theologia Moralis," III, 550.
36 Fanfani, "De Indulgentiis," 40.
37 Beringer-Hilgers, "Die Ablaesse," I, 114.
38 Beringer-Hilgers, "Die Ablaesse," I, 114.
39 Raccolta, XVI.

CHAPTER VII.

THE BENEFICIARIES OF INDULGENCES.

It is the purpose of this chapter to consider those to whom indulgences may be applied. After what has been said in explanation of the elements of the definition contained in Canon 911, very little need be added in this place.

The first class to whom indulgences may be applied are those who actually gain them. By the very nature of things, the primary beneficiaries should be those who, by complying with the prescribed conditions, gain the indulgence. This is the manifest intention of the Church, an intention the acceptance of which she takes as a matter of course. Thus in Canon 925,1: "In order that one be capable of gaining indulgences, etc.," she does not deem it necessary to point out the fact that one may gain indulgences for oneself. She assumes that fact to require no emphasis, and she immediately proceeds to lay down norms governing the gaining of indulgences for oneself. That the gainer of indulgence should be the first to benefit by it is a corollary of the thesis that the Church actually grants indulgences; and of that thesis enough has been written.

By the nature of things, too, certain classes are excluded from the beneficent operation of indulgences. The damned in hell cannot be the recipients of indulgences, because they are in a state of punishment which is eternal and which admits no mitigation either by indulgences or by any other method. For a diametrically opposite reason, indulgences cannot be applied to the Blessed in Heaven. For them the last farthing has been paid, the last vestige of punishment for past transgressions has been removed.[1]

A natural question to ask is, can one apply indulgences to others among the living? There is nothing in the nature of indulgences prohibiting such a practice. And, therefore, if it should ever seem advisable to the Supreme Pontiff, on whom rests the fixing of norms for the application of indulgences, he might so arrange that the faithful could apply indulgences to their living fellowmen.[2] Nevertheless, there is an extrinsic argument against such procedure. For the practice would undoubtedly be the occasion of promoting carelessness among that class of Christians who are already inclined to laxity. Such persons would not concern themselves about discharging the debt of temporal punishment due to their sins, nay, more, they would not refrain from committing new sins, consoling themselves with the presumption that their charitable and more zealous brethren would assume their burden and gain indulgences for them.[2a] It was a matter of prudence and expediency to forestall such an event. And this the Church did by legislating: "No one gaining indulgences can apply them to others among the living."[3]

To grant an indulgence applicable to other living persons would be "against all tradition and the constant practice of the Church. So far not a single indulgence is recorded as having been granted by the Pope to be applied 'vicariously'—to the living."[3a] What to some appeared to be an exception to this constant practice of the Church occurred when, on August 22, 1906, in response to the request of the Procurator General of the Friars Minor, the Congregation of Indulgences conceded that the plenary indulgence connected with the general absolution "non solum pro defunctis, ut auctores tenent, sed etiam pro vivis applicari possit."[3b] "Pro vivis" in this indult was interpreted as a concession to apply the indulgence to others among the living.[3c] But that interpretation was erroneous. The Procurator General of the Friars Minor had presented his petition to the Congregation to settle a doubt concerning the efficacy of the general absolution. Since Paul V recalled all personal indulgences granted to religious orders, save those given for the dead, authors had taught that the indulgence connected with the general absolution could only be applied to the departed; that it could not be kept by the gainer. That is the significance of "Ut auctores tenent" in the indult. To settle the doubt, and if necessary, to obtain a new concession, the Procurator General appealed to the Congregation of Indulgences. His intention was simply to be assured that this indulgence could be gained by the religious for themselves as well as for the Poor Souls. Nothing more than that was asked; nothing more was granted by the Congregation.[3d]

Not all indulgences are applicable to the dead, but only such as are expressly declared to be so applicable. A preceding paragraph stated that the matter of application of indulgences is wholly dependent upon the Supreme Pontiff. Hence it is for him to declare to whom indulgences may be applied. This has actually been done by appending some such expression as "defunctis tantum applicabilis," or "pro vivis et defunctis," to many briefs of the past in which indulgences were granted. Moreover, a decree of the Congregation of Indulgences declares that all those indulgences contained in the official collection, the Raccolta, may be applied to the Poor Souls.[4] Besides this, Canon 930 makes the provision that unless the contrary is clear, all indulgences granted by the Pope are applicable to the souls in Purgatory. Finally, Canon 913,2 vindicates to the Roman Pontiff the exclusive right of granting indulgences for the dead.

In order that an indulgence be actually applied to the Poor Souls, an intention to that end is required on the part of him who fulfills the conditions for gaining the indulgence. For in the ordinary course of events, the indulgence accrues to the gainer, unless other disposal is made of it. Ordinarily, therefore, an actual intention to apply an indulgence to the Poor Souls is necessary. "It is understood that an actual intention or purpose is required, in order to apply to the Poor Souls in Purgatory the indulgences which one would otherwise gain for oneself."[5] However, the heroic act obviates the need of having an actual intention to apply indulgences to the dead. For by the heroic act one voluntarily excludes oneself from gaining indulgences for oneself, and transfers all that may be gained to the Poor Souls.[5a] So long as this heroic act perseveres as an habitual intention, there is no necessity of an actual intention to apply indulgences to the departed.

NOTES ON CHAPTER VII.

1 Fanfani, "De Indulgentiis," 31.
2 Noldin, "Summa Theologiae Moralis," III, 312b; Suarez, "De Poenitentia," Disp. 52, sec. 7, 6; De Lugo, "De Poenitentia," Disp. XXVII, 77.
2a Eccles. Review, XXXIX, 201.
3 Canon 930.
3a Eccles. Review, XXXIX, 201.
3b Eccles. Review, XXXIX, 202.
3c Eccles. Review, XXXVIII, 553-555.
3d Eccles. Review, XXXIX, 202.
4 Decr. Auth. S. C. Indul. et Reliq., 261.
5 Beringer-Hilgers, "Die Ablaesse," I, 115.
5a Collectanea S. C. P. F., 1647, ad 2.

CHAPTER VIII.

Compliance with Prescribed Conditions.

The Church grants indulgences, not as absolute and free gifts, but as contingent concessions, dependent on the performance of certain works which are prescribed as conditions sine qua non. He who would gain the indulgence must comply with the conditions prescribed therefor, must perform the works to which the indulgence accrues. "In order that the subject who is capable really gain them, he must perform the works enjoined at the specified time and in the prescribed manner, according to the tenor of the concession."[1] This conditional concession is a postulate of the position which the Church occupies with reference to the treasure of satisfactions of Christ and the Saints. Christ assigned to the Church the office of dispensing these satisfactions; He did not, however, make her the prodigal dissipator of the treasure. Accordingly, it is the teaching of theologians that an indulgence cannot be licitly nor validly granted without a cause.[2]

As to the importance of the cause, St. Thomas says: "Any cause which tends to the utility of the Church and the honor of God is a sufficient reason for granting indulgences."[3]

The cause for which the indulgence is given, the work prescribed for gaining the indulgence, is but a condition. And that condition need not be, in fact, it cannot be, strictly proportionate to the indulgence. There is, however, a certain relation of congruity to be observed between the work and the indulgence, in order that the latter may be a reasonable concession. This congruity, be it noted, is not to be measured solely by the difficulty of the task imposed, but rather by the relation of the work to the end intended by the granter of the indulgence. Superficially, it would seem incongruous to attach a plenary indulgence to a work so trifling as merely placing oneself in the presence of the Holy Father in order to receive the papal blessing. But the incongruity vanishes when one's appearance before the Pope is viewed as a public profession of faith in the primacy of the Vicar of Jesus Christ and a protestation of obedience to the head of the Church.

From the stipulation that to every indulgence there must correspond some contribution, in the form of good works, on the part of the recipient, it follows that the works performed must be free works.[4] In other words, the work designated to satisfy the conditions for gaining an indulgence must not be one that is incumbent on a person in view of some law or precept. "An indulgence cannot be gained by a work to the performance of which one is bound by law or precept, unless the contrary is expressly mentioned in the concession."[5] Hence, if a day's fasting is enjoined for the indulgence, one cannot satisfy the condition by observing the Lenten fast to which the precept of the Church obliges. It is to be noted that this principle does not apply in the case of works enjoined by the rule of a religious community. Since the rule does not ordinarily bind under pain of sin, per se, prayers recited and good works performed in accordance with the rule serve to gain the indulgences connected with such prayers and good works.[5a]

Other exceptions to the general regulation are made. Canon 932 explicitly mentions some such exceptions and makes provision for others. The ecclesiastical authority may specify that the conditions demanded for gaining an indulgence may be fulfilled at one act with the performance of the same works in obedience to a precept. Thus, the Supreme Pontiff might have conceded that the hour's adoration prescribed for the indulgence of the Priests' Eucharistic League could be spent in reciting the Divine Office.

The question has been mooted among authors whether one and the same work sufficed for gaining an indulgence and acquitting the sacramental penance. The affirmative opinion seemed to predominate. And that predominance was enhanced by the well-nigh universal practice of confessors' imposing indulgenced good works as penance in the sacred tribunal.[6] Whatever theoretical discussion may have been carried on among authors, an authoritative decision of the Congregation of Indulgences upheld the opinion that indulgenced prayers imposed in penance served the twofold purpose of satisfying the penance and gaining the indulgence.[7] Canon 932 confirms this decision: "Whoever performs a work imposed in sacramental penance, which work chances to be enriched with indulgences, can at the same time satisfy the penance and gain the indulgences."

Both the decision of June 14, 1901, and Canon 932 offer a possibility of misinterpretation to the unwary reader. Superficially read, the Canon seems to imply that any work imposed as penance by the confessor can at the same time serve in fulfillment of the conditions for gaining an indulgence. Such is not the case. The Canon says: "A work enriched with indulgences," and not merely an unindulgenced work which is one of the conditions prescribed for gaining an indulgence.[8] An example will make the point clearer. Suppose that a fast of one day is prescribed as a condition of gaining the Jubilee Indulgence. Suppose that the confessor imposes a day's fast in the tribunal of penance. Then the penitent cannot satisfy his sacramental penance and gain the Jubilee Indulgence by fasting one day. Canon 932 is not intended to cover such a contingency, for this fast is not "a work enriched with indulgences." But Canon 932 does apply whenever, for instance, the confessor imposes the recitation of the Rosary or the Way of the Cross or some similar indulgenced prayer or pious work.[9] In such an event both the penance and the condition of the indulgence are satisfied by one recitation of the prayer or one performance of the good work.

Besides the sacramental penance, another exercise exempt from the general norm of Canon 932 is the Paschal Communion. In the decree of the Congregation of Indulgences of March 19, 1841, it was declared: "By Confession and Communion received on Easter, both the plenary indulgence connected with the papal blessing is gained and the Paschal precept is satisfied."[10] On May 10, 1844, the same Congregation extended the above decree—originally given in reference only to the indulgence associated with the papal blessing—so that a single reception of Holy Communion suffices to fulfill the Paschal precept and to gain *any* indulgence for which Holy Communion is prescribed.[11] However, one indulgence is excepted, that of the Jubilee. For the decision of 1844 makes the proviso: "Provided the indulgence to be gained is not in the form of the Jubilee, for which a special Confession and Communion are required."[12]

Closely allied with the question treated above is the prescription of the latter part of Canon 933: "By one and the same work to which indulgences have been annexed on various titles, several indulgences cannot be gained, unless the prescribed work is Confession or Communion, or unless it is expressly provided otherwise." In general, a distinct repetition of the exercise is required for gaining each of the indulgences that have been attached to it. To illustrate: An indulgence of fifty days is granted for signing oneself with the Sign of the Cross.[12a] Suppose a rescript were issued by which an indulgence of fifty days could be gained for every act of piety performed in the Church of St. Gertrude. One might conclude that making the Sign of the Cross in the Church of St. Gertrude would suffice to gain both the indulgences of fifty days, a total of one hundred days. But the law stated in Canon 933 excludes that conclusion.

The same Canon excepts Confession and Communion from the general rule that only one indulgence can be gained by one performance of the prescribed work. An illustration will show the effect of that exception to the law. A plenary indulgence may be gained by those who recite the prayer "En ego" before an image of the Crucified, on condition of having confessed and received Holy Communion. By the concession of Pius X on June 25, 1914, a plenary indulgence is granted to all the faithful who, having confessed and received Holy Communion, visit a church on the second of November and pray for the Holy Father's intention. Suppose a communicant on All Souls' Day desires to gain the plenary indulgence with which the prayer "En ego" is enriched. Does he by so doing forfeit the opportunity of gaining the other plenary indulgences during the day? Manifestly he cannot receive Holy Communion again; yet Communion is a condition of the toties quoties indulgence. Here the words of Canon 933 serve the purpose of enabling the communicant to gain both indulgences by one Confession and Communion. The same is the case with all indulgences for which Confession and Communion are prescribed.[13]

The Canon quoted above provides that the competent authorities may stipulate that more than one indulgence may be gained by one and the same work.[14]

It is for the competent authority to determine the conditions under which the treasure of the Church is to be distributed. It is within the competence of that authority to adapt those conditions to circumstances. If circumstances warrant, there is nothing to prevent the authority's permitting the cumulation of indulgences. It is well to note, however, that Canon 913,3 denies the Pope's inferior the power of indulgencing objects already indulgenced by the Pope or by another prelate. Since, for example, the making of the Sign of the Cross has been indulgenced by the Holy See, no Bishop can attach an additional indulgence to that pious exercise, unless he prescribes new conditions; for instance, he may add an indulgence of fifty days for making the Sign of the Cross while kneeling.[15]

Instances are not lacking in which the Supreme Pontiffs have explicitly declared that one and the same work of piety should avail for gaining several indulgences. A notable example is the decree of the Congregation of Indulgences, in virtue of which a single recitation of the beads suffices to gain both the Crozier indulgence and the indulgence of the Dominican Rosary.[16] A more recent instance is recorded in the present pontificate. The Sacred Penitentiary prefaced the list of Apostolic Indulgences granted by Pius XI with four remarks, the last of which reads: "By an express declaration of our Holy Father, the present concession of Apostolic Indulgences does not derogate in the least from the indulgences which other Pontiffs may have attached to the prayers, pious exercises, or works enumerated below."[17] On June 14, 1922, the Sacred Tribunal answered a doubt proposed to it, the effect of the answer being that this fourth remark prefaced to the list of Apostolic Indulgences really amounted to an "express provision to the contrary" demanded by Canon 933,3, so that one performance of one of the works in the list sufficed to gain several indulgences.[18] The consequence of this concession is that by one recitation of the Angelus, for example, one gains both the indulgence applied thereto in the Raccolta [19] and also the Apostolic Indulgence of one hundred days.[20] The same applies to all other acts of piety enumerated in the list of Pius XI to which previous Pontiffs have attached indulgences.

The work performed in gaining an indulgence must be morally good, not only as to its substance—it will always be that, since it is inconceivable that the granter of an indulgence would demand the performance of a morally vicious act—but also in its circumstances. There is unanimous agreement among authors that an act vitiated by circumstances that are mortally sinful cannot serve to gain an indulgence. Thus, to bestow an alms on a poor family with the purpose of inducing them to abandon the faith could not merit indulgence, but reprobation instead. Theologians differ as to whether works performed under venially sinful circumstances fulfill the requirements for gaining an indulgence. Among others, Suarez [21] teaches the sufficiency of an act venially sinful because of a bad end or bad circumstances, provided, however, the evil circumstances do not totally corrupt the act. Hence he considers sufficient a prayer said with distractions, a good work done with vain-glory, not only as its accompaniment, but even as its partial motive.[22] St. Alphonsus calls this opinion of Suarez "communis."[22a]

The works assigned for the gaining of an indulgence must be performed in their moral entirety.[23] Omissions through ignorance, substitutions made in good faith or for apparently cogent reasons, disregard of the conditions for whatever cause, all these result in the forfeiture of the indulgence. The reason is apparent. Indulgences are free gifts so far as the recipients are concerned. It is within the power of the giver to make them dependent on whatever conditions he deems expedient. And no injustice is done if the gift is withheld from one who does not comply with the conditions, even though his non-compliance be inculpable.[24]

"Opus debet moraliter totum adimpleri," says Vermeersch.[25] This but re-echoes Canon 925,2: "In order that the subject who is capable really gain them (sc, indulgences), he must perform the works enjoined, according to the tenor of the concession." Since, however, the dictum of the moralists, "parum pro nihilo reputatur," applies also to indulgences, a trifling omission will not prevent the gaining of the indulgence. Just what constitutes "parvitas materiae" in this department cannot be determined with accuracy, nor can a universally applicable standard be set up. The part of the work that may be omitted without frustrating the indulgence will differ in each case, because the total amount demanded in each case differs. Even in specific instances, authors are not agreed on the amount that may be omitted with impunity. To cite but one example of divergence of opinion: In the recitation of the Rosary, Fanfani thinks that the omission of four or five Aves would not prevent the indulgence,[26] whereas Vermeersch says to omit more than two or three would prevent,[27] and Melata [28] and Beringer [28a] say to omit more than one or two Aves frustrates the indulgence.

While the performance of the works exactly as prescribed is required in general, the Church has provided for the commutation of these works on the authority of confessors. Pope Benedict XIV, in conferring faculties on the minor penitentiaries who were to expedite the hearing of Confessions during the Jubilee of

1750, empowered these confessors to reduce the fifteen prescribed visits of the Basilicas to three visits or to some other pious works in the case of pilgrims to Rome; to commute the thirty visits enjoined on native Romans to other acts of piety adapted to their capacity.[29]

Again, members of various confraternities have from time to time been made the beneficiaries of the power conferred on confessors to commute the pious works to which indulgences were attached. Such a favor was granted to the Rosary Confraternity in 1773, in consequence of which confessors could commute those indulgenced works which exposed the performers to the danger of persecution.[30] A decree of the Congregation of Indulgences of February 25, 1877, substantially repeated on July 16, 1887, granted to all confraternities the favor that members who were sick or otherwise detained might have the condition of visiting a church commuted into other pious works by their confessors, provided each sodality had separate recourse to the Holy See for the favor.[31] On another occasion, a petition was presented to the Holy Father on behalf of the sick who, unable to comply with the condition of receiving Holy Communion and visiting a church, were deprived of many indulgences. And on September 18, 1862, it was conceded that confessors might commute the prescribed Communion and visit into other pious works.[32] Finally, Canon 935 gives to all confessors the general faculty of commuting the works required for gaining an indulgence, the faculty to be exercised in behalf of those whom a legitimate impediment prevents from doing the enjoined works.

The conditions for gaining an indulgence can be commuted by any priest who is approved for Confessions. However, in view of the decree of the Congregation for the Propagation of the Faith, dated February 20, 1801,[33] authors teach that this faculty may be exercised outside the confessional.[34] And that opinion is strengthened by the fact that Canon 935 empowers "confessarii" to commute, making no such restriction as "in actu tantum confessionis."

The good works must be done in person by the one gaining the indulgence.[35] It is but reasonable that it should be so. For the indulgence is granted, not in view of personal worth or dignity, but in view of compliance with the conditions laid down. The indulgence becomes mine in consequence of my fulfilling the conditions.[36] In the case of alms-giving, however, an exception is made, whereby one may employ an agent to distribute the alms in one's name. Vermeersch goes further, demanding only that one know and consent to alms being given in one's name, even though the alms be not one's own property.[37] The same contention is made by Bastien, at least in reference to the gaining of the Jubilee Indulgence, which, incidentally, is the chief indulgence with which alms-giving is associated as a condition.[38]

A case similar to the above is the recitation of public prayers. Personal compliance with the conditions for the indulgence was mitigated by the Congregation of Indulgences, to the extent that alternate recitation of the public prayer sufficed to gain the indulgence.[39] Canon 934,3 extends this concession of the Congregation, stipulating that not only alternate recitation with a companion suffices, but that it is enough to attend in silence while another recites. Canon 936 makes a similar concession in favor of deaf mutes. In gaining the indulgence for the Way of the Cross it has been conceded that in a large concourse of people it is not necessary for each one to meet the requirement of moving from place to place, but that the condition of local motion is complied with when a priest and two clerics or chanters go about from station to station, alternating with the congregation in the recitation of the customary prayers.[40] In an answer of the Congregation of Indulgences of February 27, 1901, it was granted that the method of making the Way of the Cross described above might be followed in the chapels of religious houses "ob loci angustiam," and that instead of the priest and two clerics or chanters, one brother, not necessarily a priest, could go from Station to Station, reciting the prayers.[40a] Similarly, on January 22, 1858, Pope Pius IX conceded that holding the chaplet in hand—a condition prescribed for gaining the Rosary Indulgences—might be dispensed with when the beads are said in common, the condition being sufficiently observed if only one of the community holds the chaplet and the rest join in the prayer.[41]

NOTES ON CHAPTER VIII.

1 Canon 925, 2.
2 Vermeersch, "Epitome Juris Canonici," II, 202.
3 Commentarium in Quattuor Sententias, Disp. XX, q. 1, art. 3.
4 Melata, "Manuale de Indulgentiis," 29.
5 Canon 932.
5a Beringer-Steinen, "Die Ablaesse," I, 95.
6 Amort, "Historia Indulgentarum," II, 33; Maurel, "Le cretien eclaire sur la nature et l'usage des indulgences," 92.
7 Collectanea S. C. P. F., 2116.
8 Melata, "Manuale de Indulgentiis," 51.
9 Benedict XIV, const. "Inter Praeteritos," 53.
10 Decr. Auth. S. C. Indul. et Reliq., 228.
11 Decr. Auth. S. C. Indul. et Reliq., 327.
12 Decr. Auth. S. C. Indul. et Reliq., 327.
12a Raccolta, 16.
13 Decr. Auth. S. C. Indul. et Reliq., 291.
14 Canon 933.
15 Decr. Auth. S. C. Indul. et Reliq., 433, ad 1 et 4.
16 Acta Sanctae Sedis, XL, 442.
17 Acta Apost. Sedis, XIV, 143.
18 Acta Apost. Sedis, XIV, 394.
19 Raccolta, 92.
20 Acta Apost. Sedis, XIV, 143.
21 De Sacramento Poenitentiae, Disp. LII, sec. ii, 3.
22 Vermeersch, "Epitome Juris Canonici," II, 215.
22a St. Alphonsus, "Theologia Moralis," VI, 533.
23 Vermeersch, "Epitome Juris Canonici," II, 215.
24 Fanfani, "De Indulgentiis," 41.

25 Vermeersch, "Epitome Juris Canonici, II, 215.
26 Fanfani, "De Indulgentiis," 41.
27 Vermeersch, "Epitome Juris Canonici," II, 215, 4.
28 Melata, "Manuale de Indulgentiis," 45.
28a Beringer-Steinen, "Die Ablaesse," I, 92.
29 Benedict XIV, const. "Convocatis," XX; "Inter Praeteritos," LIII.
30 Collectanea S. C. P. F., 499.
31 Decr. Auth. S. C. Indul. et Reliq., 431.
32 Decr. Auth. S. C. Indul. et Reliq., 393.
33 Collectanea S. C. P. F., 657.
34 Vermeersch, "Epitome Juris Canonici," II, 221; Sabetti-Barrett, "Compendium Theologiae Moralis," 1050, q. 17.
35 Raccolta, XVII.
36 Melata, "Manual de Indulgentiis," 47.
37 Vermeersch, "Epitome Juris Canonici," II, 215.
38 Bastien, "Tractatus de Jubilaeo Anni Sancti," 110.
39 Decr. Auth. S. C. Indul. et Reliq., 249, ad 2.
40 Decr. Auth. S. C. Indul. et Reliq., 210.
40a Analecta Ecclesiastica, IX, 81.
41 Decr. Auth. S. C. Indul. et. Reliq., 384.

CHAPTER IX.

PARTICULAR WORKS.

Thus far the conditions associated with indulgences have been treated in a general way. Something remains to be said about certain conditions in particular. The conditions usually imposed are four in number; I. the recitation of prayers, II. Confession, III. Communion, IV. visiting of churches. Incidentally these are the conditions understood in the formula "under the usual conditions," which formula is added to many concessions of plenary indulgences.[1] However, circumstances sometimes indicate that a visit to a church is not included in that formula, but that Confession, Communion, and prayer for the Pope's intention are the "Debitae conditiones."[1a]

1. Prayer in one form or other is practically always demanded as a condition for gaining indulgences. It is unnecessary here to speak of the qualities of prayer, to treat of the virtual intention required to pray, of the superficial, literal, and spiritual attention, without which prayer is not a human act nor a service to God, not a condition sufficient for indulgences.

When prayers are assigned for the gaining of an indulgence, those prayers must be recited orally, at least in part, unless provision to the contrary is made. Canon 934,1 explicitly requires vocal prayer when it is for the Pope's intention; "If prayer for the intention of the Supreme Pontiff is prescribed for the gaining of indulgences, mere mental prayer is not sufficient." This Canon succinctly states what had previously been contained in a decision of the Congregation of Indulgences.[1b]

Canon 936 enables deaf mutes to gain indulgences attached to public prayers, by merely mingling with the faithful and piously meditating. As to private prayers, the same Canon permits deaf mutes to recite these prayers mentally, to express them by means of signs, or merely to read them through by running their eyes over the printed page. The part of the Canon regulating the private devotions of deaf mutes alters the former legislation contained in a decision of the Congregation of Indulgences of March 15, 1858,[2] in which it was prescribed that confessors should commute prayers to other good works in the case of deaf mutes. This power of commuting must now be restricted in accordance with Canon 935, by which confessors may commute indulgenced works only in the case of "those who are bound by a legitimate impediment." Hence, confessors may commute prayers only in the case of those deaf mutes who can neither read by sight, express in signs, nor mentally recall their prayers. For these alone are "legitimo detenti impedimento."

The Way of the Cross is an exercise sui generis in that no vocal prayer, but only mental prayer or meditation, is prescribed for gaining the indulgences. Pope Clement XII published certain rules governing this devotion, of which the sixth stated that in the private recitation of the Stations, it was not necessary to recite six Paters and Aves at each Station, as some had thought, but that it suffices to meditate, however briefly, on the Passion of our Lord, "for this is the work enjoined for gaining the indulgences."[3] Again on June 2, 1838, the Congregation of Indulgences declared that the recitation of the Pater and Ave at each Station was not a necessary condition for gaining the indulgences of the Way of the Cross.[4]

The Rosary Indulgence, besides requiring that the Paters and Aves be recited orally, demands also that meditation be made on the mysteries of the Incarnation and Redemption.[5] Such is the tenor of a decision of the Congregation of Indulgences of July 1, 1839, and of another issued on August 13, 1726.[6] In the latter instance it was asked whether one gained the indulgences by meditating on the four last things. The Sacred Congregation answered: "Non lucrari."[7] The decision of 1839 stated that meditation on the mysteries of Redemption was required to gain the indulgences of the Dominican Rosary, but not for those of the Brigitine Rosary, nor for the Apostolic Indulgences.[8] However, according to the constitution "Pretiosus" of Benedict XIII, issued May 26, 1727, illiterate persons who do not know how to meditate may gain the Rosary indulgence by merely reciting the prescribed prayers with devotion. But the Pope declared it to be his will that such persons gradually acquaint themselves with the practice of meditating on the mysteries of the Rosary.[9]

No special bodily posture is required to render a prayer apt for gaining indulgences. However, if the rescript in which the indulgence is granted specifies that the prayers be said kneeling, the condition must be observed.[10] For the benefit of those injured in the World War, Pope Benedict XV declared, on October 22, 1917, that "Indulgences, for the gaining of which were prescribed prayers and physical actions which the maimed could not perform, could be gained by the maimed if they only recited the prayers."[11]

The principle that the works assigned must be performed exactly as prescribed applies, of course, to prayers. Canon 934,2 expresses the law thus: "Indulgences cease entirely through any addition, diminution, or interpolation " "Quod satis severe intelligitur," is the comment of Vermeersch.[12]. Thus, a decision of the Sacred Penitentiary, on July 21, 1919, declared the indulgences forfeited if, in the chanting of the Litany of Loretto, the Kyrie eleison were chanted but once, or the invocation "Ora pro nobis" were not added to each title.[13] This decision was substantially repeated in 1920.[13a]

A famous instance of interpolating prescribed prayers was had in the Rosary. In certain localities, it was a practice of long standing [14] to insert in each Hail Mary, after the Holy Name, the respective mystery, "Who sweat Blood for us," "Who arose from the dead, etc." On July 1, 1839, the Congregation of Indulgences declared that such insertion of the mystery was not necessary to gain the indulgences, but said nothing about the forfeiture of the indulgences by reason of the interpolation.[15] Twenty years later, the practice having shown itself conspicuously among German-speaking Catholics, the question was raised concerning the effect of the usage on the Rosary indulgences. In 1859 Pius IX issued an indult declaring that "in the diocese of Breslau and in other places where the usage ("mos") of making the insertion prevailed," the indulgences were not lost.[15a] Being asked in July, 1920, whether the custom might be preserved and propagated, the Sacred Penitentiary gave a negative answer.[16] The scope of this answer was subsequently explained when the same tribunal declared that the former indult of Pius IX was in no wise revoked by Canon 934,2.[16x] In other words, the Penitentiary did not repudiate the practice of interpolating, wherever it prevailed; but the practice was not to be extended.[16a] Finally on January 22, 1921, the Sacred Penitentiary issued a new indult, permitting this interpolation of the Hail Mary, without prejudice to the Rosary indulgence, for all those among whom the practice prevailed in 1921.[17]

Vermeersch asks whether this insertion of the mystery is prejudicial to the Rosary indulgence, even in the absence of an indult. His answer is that if one's intention is not to effect the integrity of the Hail Mary, but merely to introduce a pause during which the mystery is recalled, there is no danger of losing the indulgence.[18] In proof he alleges the validity of Baptism conferred "In the name of the Father and of the Son and of the Holy Ghost and of the Blessed Virgin; provided he who baptizes does not intend to number the Blessed Virgin with the three Divine Persons." If, he argues, in the more important matter of Baptism the interpolation is no obstacle to the validity of the Sacrament, a fortiori it is no impediment in the less important matter of indulgences. The analogy between Baptism and indulgences in this respect is not apparent. The sacramental form of Baptism has been specifically determined by Christ.[19] The Church lacks authority to declare invalid a form which conforms essentially to that instituted by Christ. But in the matter of indulgences, the Church is the final arbiter. She can declare insufficient any formula of prayer which, by reason of an interpolation, recedes even accidentally from the appointed version. This power the Church asserts in Canon 934,2. That Canon contains no indication of an intention to exempt the Rosary from the general law by permitting an interpolation in its component prayers. Now, if the Canon rejects interpolations, and if there is no indult permitting them, it is difficult to concede with Vermeersch that the indulgence is not lost by the interpolation. Besides, one wonders why both Pius IX and Benedict XV should have taken the pains of issuing two indults sanctioning a practice which, if Vermeersch's argument be valid, needed no sanction. Why should the Sacred Penitentiary have assumed the inconvenience of apparently correcting an oversight on its part, and declaring that the indult of Pius IX was not abrogated by one of its former decisions, if, after all, the indult and the abrogation of the indult were not matters of practical consequence?

In reference to our own country, it seems certain that the practice of thus interpolating the Hail Mary does not jeopardize the Rosary indulgence. The argument adduced against the practice is that the indult of 1859 and the indult of 1921 expressed tolerance of the *custom* of reciting the mystery after the Holy Name. But a juridical custom in the matter was never established in the United States, since no entire American diocese adhered to the practice.[20] And it is common law that no secular community smaller than a diocese can become the subject of a canonical custom.[21] It is to be noted, however, that the question of *custom* has no place whatever in the discussion. The indult of Pius IX did not approve a *custom;* it said "In the diocese of Breslau and in places where the practice ("mos," not "consuetudo") prevailed."[21a] Likewise, the general indult of January 22, 1921, is "for the extension of the same indult in favor of all those who, in any place whatsoever, are wont to recite the Rosary according to the above-mentioned manner ("morem," not "consuetudinem").[21b] The "stylus curiae" never uses "mos" in the meaning of a juridical custom. Hence the two indults in question were dealing, not with a canonical custom, but, what is wholly different, with a popular practice, at most a "consuetudo facti." Now, while it is true that parishes cannot establish a canonical custom,[21c] ("consuetudo juris"), there is nothing to prohibit their establishing a practice or usage ("mos"). It is a matter of common knowledge that many parishes in the United States adhered to the practice of inserting the mystery into the Hail Mary.

The indult of 1921 permits this usage without forfeiture of the indulgences (in America as elsewhere) *wherever it prevailed in 1921,* for the words of the indult are: "for the extension of the same indult in favor of all those who, in any place whatsoever, are wont to recite the Rosary according to the above-mentioned mánner."[21d]

An indulgence is not lost if the indulgenced prayer is translated into another language. Hence, no matter in what tongue the prayer is recited, the indulgence can be gained. However, precaution must be taken that the version is true to the original. This precaution will consist in the declaration either of the Sacred Penitentiary of a local Ordinary where the language of the translation is in general use.[22] Vermeersch sees in this enactment of Canon 934,2, an advance over the old legislation. He says: "Under the old law, only the condition of faithful translation was demanded as essential (Decreta Authentica No. 415). But now the published version must have the attestation of faithful translation from the Sacred Penitentiary or from a competent Ordinary. But in the case of a manuscript version, we think it suffices if the translation is faithful; for it is not customary to ask an authentication of manuscripts."[23] The author cites No. 415 of the Authentic Decrees of the Congregation of Indulgences in proof that of old each individual might verify the translation to his own satisfaction, no intervention of ecclesiastical authority being required. But he evidently overlooked the concluding sentence of the decree which he cites. For that concluding sentence is substantially identical with Canon 934,2, in which private verification of versions of indulgenced prayers receives no recognition. Whether the learned author's distinction between "versio manuscripta" and "versio typis edita" is well made, whether the authoritative authentication of the latter is not required, are matters not above question. Beringer cites Vermeersch's opinion, qualifying it to the extent that a person using his own unauthenticated—though correct—manuscript version of a prayer would gain the indulgence.[23a] Canon 934,2 makes no distinction between versions for private use and published translations. The Canon simply demands that the prayer be recited in a version the fidelity of which has been authenticated. And the only means of authenticating the translation—whether private or public—which the law knows is that set down in Canon 934: the declaration of the Penitentiary or of a competent Ordinary.

For gaining indulgences, prayer for the Pope's intention is often prescribed. Obviously, the "intentio Pontificis" refers to the mind of the Pope, not as an individual, but to the purposes that are near his heart as the Vicar of Christ and the visible head of the Church. Those purposes theologians enumerate as the exaltation of the Church, the extirpation of heresy, the propagation of the faith, the conversion of sinners, and concord among Christian princes.[24] There need be no uneasiness as to which of these intentions one should pray for, since the general intention of praying for the Pope's mind, or even the mere will to gain indulgences, is sufficient. Thus runs an answer of the Congregation of Indulgences to the question: "When, for the gaining of indulgences, prayer for a specified end is prescribed, e.g., for the extirpation of heresy, is it necessary to have an explicit intention, expressed each time? The Congregation answered: Negative."[25]

What manner and what amount of prayer fulfills this prescription? Canon 934,1 gives the answer: "If for the gaining of indulgences, prayer for the intention of the Supreme Pontiff is prescribed, mere mental prayer does not suffice; the selection of the vocal prayer is left to the choice of the faithful, unless a particular prayer is assigned." Nothing need be said here in explanation of the requirements of vocal prayer, nor of cases in which a definite prayer has been appointed; for these subjects have been previously noted. The Canon just quoted leaves to the pious discretion of individuals the selection of the prayer and the determination of the amount. Commentators before and since the Code have freely speculated on what would be a becoming amount of prayer. A definite decision has not been reached, but with practical unanamity the authors fix five Paters and Aves, or their equivalent, as an amount certainly sufficient. Thus Fanfani: "The prayer is not to be too brief, especially if there is question of a plenary indulgence; five or six Paters and Aves, or equivalent, are certainly sufficient."[26] Vermeersch, referring to the authority of St. Alphonsus, Mocchegiani, and Beringer, says: "Since the law demands merely prayer, not a few think that one Pater is enough. Not a few think that a prayer so brief shows lack of devotion which would prevent the gaining of a plenary indulgence. That five Paters and Aves, or a prayer equivalent to these, suffice, is clearly evident."[27] Pruemmer reaches a similar conclusion, adding that some authors think a shorter prayer sufficient.[28] Noldin adds the following: "It cannot be shown by any argument that five Paters and Aves are required. On the contrary, there can be no doubt that under the New Code one Pater suffices to gain the indulgence."[29] And this opinion of Noldin seems acceptable. The only argument favoring the necessity of more than one Pater as minimum is that referred to, though not adopted, by Vermeersch, namely: "A prayer so brief shows lack of devotion."[30] And this lack of devotion is not at all palpably shown in thus abbreviating the prayer. For instance, the Church grants a plenary indulgence at the hour of death, prescribing no longer prayer than the repetition of the Holy Name. If the Church does not evince a defect of devotion in prescribing so brief a prayer, how can the faithful be convicted of lack of devotion if they choose one of equal brevity? Strictly speaking, therefore, it would appear that any formula, even monosyllabic, provided it be a true prayer and be vocal, satisfies the condition. This, however, is not to advocate rejection of the time-honored practice sanctioning the five Paters and Aves. It is merely intended to show that a much shorter prayer may suffice. Certainly the decisions rendered by the Congregation of Indulgences on May 29, 1841,[31] and on September 13, 1888,[32] and Canon 934,1, do not weaken the contention that a prayer less lengthy than five Paters and Aves is sufficient.

II. Confession is a condition often connected with the gaining of indulgences. And it is an indispensable condition whenever called for by the document of concession, according to the provisions to be enumerated in the following paragraphs. However, if no express mention of Confession is made in the rescript of indulgence, it is not required, even of those in mortal sin. But this question has been treated in a previous chapter.

One of the first questions to suggest itself in this connection concerns the necessity of Confession as a condition for indulgences, when one is not conscious of a mortal sin. A decision rendered by the Congregation of Indulgences on May 19, 1759 peremptorily demands Confession even in such cases, if the concession prescribes Confession as a condition.[33] But in this contingency it is not necessary that the penitent receive absolution in order to gain the indulgence. So says

Vermeersch,[34] citing a decision of May 6, 1852.[35] It is also well to note that in virtue of an indult of December 9, 1763,[36] those who habitually confess weekly and who are not conscious of mortal sin may omit a special Confession prescribed for gaining any indulgence, excepting the Jubilee.[37]

In gaining several plenary indulgences on the same day, for each of which Confession is a condition, it is not the mind of the Church to insist on confessing more than once in a single day. The Congregation of Indulgences so decided, giving as its reason that it is not customary to repeat Confession so frequently.[38] Similarly, Canon 933 excepts Confession from the general rule that several indulgences cannot be gained by one and the same work to which a number of indulgences have been attached.

The time within which the Confession may be made has occasioned some uncertainty in the past. Originally fixed to the very day on which the indulgence was to be gained, by a decision of the Congregation of Indulgences it was conceded that the Confession might be made on the vigil of that day.[39] Next, the indult of 1763 was issued, the effect of which was to extend the time to the last preceding regular Confession in the case of those who confessed weekly.[40] On June 12, 1822, the time was extended to one week preceding the indulgenced feast.[41] This extension was in favor of all the faithful, irrespective of the frequency of their Confessions, and embraced all indulgences except the Jubilee. Subsequently, it was declared that the wording of the decree of 1822 "infra hebdomadam" meant the eight days immediately preceding the feast, and did not refer to the last complete week preceding that day. In other words, the faithful—excluding, of course, those who confessed weekly, and for whom the indult of 1763 provided—could not, in virtue of the Confession made on Sunday, gain the indulgences of a feast that fell on Saturday of the succeeding week, interposing thirteen days between the Confession and the feast. Also, declaration was made that this Confession sufficed for gaining as many indulgences as occurred during the intervening eight days.[42] On October 6, 1870, a decree set forth that the eight-day anticipation of Confession was applicable not only to feast days, but also to other occasions on which indulgences were granted because of some solemnity.[43]

Canon 931 reiterates some of the former regulations and enlarges the scope of others: "The Confession prescribed for gaining any indulgences can be made within the eight days which immediately precede *the day to which* the indulgence *is assigned;*—both (Confession and Communion) can be made within the entire octave that follows (that day)." The first part of the paragraph just read is but a summary of the decrees emanating from the Congregation of Indulgences on December 9, 1763; June 12, 1822; and October 6, 1870. The extension of the tempus utile to the octave of the indulgenced feast is the work of the Code. New also is the second paragraph of Canon 931: "Likewise, for gaining the indulgences granted for pious exercises of three days' or a week's duration, etc., Confession and Communion can be made within the octave immediately following the completion of the exercise." In virtue of this legislation, the Confession demanded for gaining the indulgences of a triduum, spiritual retreat, or mission, may be made on any day within the octave immediately following the close of the respective exercise.

May the Confession associated with such devout exercises of more than one day's duration also be made eight days before the date of opening? The second paragraph of Canon 931 make no reference to the octave preceding. The norm must therefore be sought in the first paragraph. But Canon 931,1 mentions the day, not the group of days, to which an indulgence is attached; the Confession must be made within eight days immediately preceding the indulgeced day. As a rule the plenary indulgence granted for the making of tridua, retreats, missions, etc., accrues on the completion of the last exercise, the closing of the retreat, etc. In other words, the last day of the triduum is the indulgenced day. Hence a Confession made eight days before the opening date, or at any time more than eight days removed from the close of the exercise, seems insufficient.

The decree issued by the Congregation of. Indulgences on December 9, 1763, confined the concession it contained to those who were weekly penitents.[44] Canon 931,3 legislates in favor of those who habitually confess at least twice a month. Incidentally, this legislation of the Code was anticipated in a particular indult of April 4, 1879, in favor of the Kingdom of Prussia and the Diocese of Freiburg.[44a] This law eliminates the necessity of bi-weekly penitents' confessing specially each time Confession is prescribed for gaining an indulgence. "Unless they are legitimately prevented," says Canon 931,3. Therefore one is enabled to enjoy this privilege, even though on rare occasions unavoidable obstacles render semi-monthly Confession impossible.

Canon 931,3 contains another concession, first granted by Pius X through a decree of the Congregation of Indulgences of February 14, 1906.[44b] "The faithful who are wont to receive Holy Communion daily, though they fail to receive the one or other time in the week, can gain all indulgences, even without making the Confession which would otherwise be necessary for gaining them." Accordingly, daily communicants are not obliged to make the prescribed Confession in order to gain indulgences. And by daily communicants are here meant those who receive daily or nearly so, who receive at least five times a week: "though they fail to receive the one or other time in the week." And it is noteworthy that communicants enjoy this favor, no matter what reason, or lack of cause, induces them to absent themselves from the Holy Table once or twice a week. For the word of the law is "abstineant," not "legitime impediantur," as is the case in bi-weekly Confession regulated by Canon 931,3. Moreover it will be noted that the Canon is disjunctive, reading: "Those who are wont to approach the Sacrament of Penance *or* ("aut") to receive Holy Communion." Therefore the Canon benefits the man who confesses twice a month, irrespective of the frequency of his Communions; it also benefits his neighbor who habitually communicates at least five times a week, whether he confesses bi-weekly or less frequently.[45] The indulgence of the Jubilee is excepted from this regulation.

The distinction between the three paragraphs of Canon 931 must ever be borne in mind. Insofar as they appertain to Confession—their relation to Communuion will be treated presently—the first paragraph refers to the requirement of Confession whenever the indulgence is granted for a particular day. This requirement is met if the Confession is made eight days before or after the respective date, whether the person in question be a frequent and regular penitent and communicant or not. The second paragraph differs from the first only insofar as the indulgence referred to in the second paragraph is granted, not for a single day, but for an exercise of more than one day's duration. The Confession required for such indulgences may be made eight days before or after the closing exercise, but not eight days before the opening date. The third paragraph grants that two distinct classes of Catholics, namely those who are bi-weekly penitents and those who receive Communion daily or nearly so, are exempted from making the Confession otherwise prescribed for the gaining of any indulgence, the Jubilee excepted.

III. It is the usual practice to prescribe Communion as a condition for gaining an indulgence whenever Confession is demanded. To satisfy this prescription the reception of Communion must be in conformity with certain requirements. These are three in number; the Communion must be sacramental, spiritual Communion being insufficient; it must be worthy, to the exclusion of a sacrilegious Communion; it must be received within the proper time.[46] The first two conditions are too evident to require comment here. Concerning the time within which the Communion must be received, a few observations will be in order.

Holy Communion need not be received on the very day of the indulgence. It may be received on the vigil of that day, and at any time within the octave immediately following. For such is the enactment of Canon 931,1. Canon 931,2 legislates to the effect that the Communion may be received during the octave following a triduum or similar pious exercise. The third paragraph of Canon 931, though referring at length to Holy Communion, does so only insofar as frequency of Communion bears on the necessity of Confession required for indulgences. That paragraph lays down no regulation touching Communion as a requirement for indulgences.

After the observations made on Canon 931 in the preceding section, it need be merely repeated here that one Holy Communion serves to gain all the indulgences granted for any day.[46a] Likewise the point has been amply emphasized that a single Communion serves both to comply with the Paschal precept and to gain any indulgence whatsoever for which Communion is a condition. That the Jubilee Indulgence constitutes an exception to this rule has also been noted in another place.

The question might arise: In what place must the Communion be received? No particular place is of obligation, and Communion received in the sick-chamber is as well suited to the end as that received in Church. If, however, both Communion and a visit to the Church are conditions, one might ask whether the two must be performed separately, or whether they may be performed simultaneously. One is at complete liberty in the matter. Fanfani has the following to say: "If a visit to a determined church is prescribed for gaining an indulgence, Holy Communion need not necessarily be received there. But if Communion is received in that church, it is not necessary to make an additional visit, provided the person is in the church at the time designated for gaining the indulgence, and recites the prescribed prayers."[47] The decision of the Congregation of Indulgences, rendered in reference to the gaining of the Portiuncula Indulgence, confirms this conclusion.[48]

In a preceding paragraph the confessor's power of commutation was treated. In reference to the commutation of Holy Communion, Pruemmer makes a statement which seems open to question. He says: "In the case of children who have not been admitted to Holy Communion, he (the confessor) cannot commute the obligation of receiving Communion to some other work, except in gaining the Jubilee."[49] The learned author gives no proof of the assertion. In the same paragraph he cites a decree of the Congregation of Indulgences of September 18, 1862, by which confessors were empowered to commute into other pious works the prescribed Communion or visits to churches in the case of those who, "by reason of protracted infirmity or other physical impediment (e.g., those in prison, those making an ocean voyage, etc.) cannot receive."[50] This concession of 1862 was made lest such unfortunate persons be deprived of many indulgences. The reason obtains in the case of children not yet admitted to the Holy Table. And Pope Benedict XIV seemingly took cognizance of that reason when he wrote into the constitution "Convocatis" the provision that confessors might substitute some other pious work for the prescribed Jubilee Communion in the case of all children who had not received their first Communion, and who would not receive it during the year of Jubilee.[51] With these arguments of fitness favoring the children, with no authoritative decision to the contrary, and above all, with Canon 935 making the unqualified provision that confessors may commute prescribed works for all "who are prevented by a legitimate impediment," it is not clear why Pruemmer withholds from confessors the power of commuting the Communion of children who have not made their first Communion.

IV. In the concession of very many indulgences, a visit to a church is demanded as a necessary condition. Visiting the church implies, in this connection, entering the sacred edifice with the intention of paying honor to God. Merely stepping into the building to escape the inclemency of the weather or to inspect the architecture or painting would not be considered an act of worship, and would not satisfy the requirements.[52] However, in the absence of a prescription to the contrary, it is not required that any prayers be recited on the occasion of the visit. For entering the church with the proper intention is itself an act of worship.[53]

However, practically all briefs in which a visit to a church is demanded, at the same time prescribe the recitation of some prayers for the Pope's intention.

Circumstances may arise in which ingress to the church is impeded. It may happen that the throng of worshippers crowds the church to the very portals, or that the doors are locked. In such an event, authors agree that the condition is fulfilled by approaching as nearly as possible to the doors of the church. This is all the more true in case one is so united with the body of the faithful filling the edifice as to be morally present at the function going on within the walls.[54]

The visit must be made in a church or public oratory. In explaining this requirement, Vermeersch refers to the definition of a public oratory as contained in Canon 1188,2, and rightly observes that the public character of an oratory does not depend on its having an entrance on a public thoroughfare, but on the circumstance that all the faithful have the right of entering it.[55] When, therefore, a visit to an undetermined church or oratory is demanded, the visit must be made in a church or oratory to which all the faithful have legitimate access. Hence the oratories of monasteries, seminaries, hospitals, etc., are not suitable for making the visits.[56]

In Canon 929 is contained a restriction of the general rule that indulgenced visits may not be made in any save a public oratory. For according to that Canon all persons living a common life in pursuit of perfection or engaged in study, or those confined by ill health in houses erected with the Ordinary's consent, which houses lack a church or public oratory; also all persons engaged in the maintenance of such establishments, may make the prescribed visits in the chapels of such houses, in which they are wont to satisfy the obligation of hearing Mass. The Canon is but an incorporation of the decision of the Holy Office approved by Pius X on January 4, 1909.[57]

As to the extent of the privileges just mentioned, it is well to note that in some indulgences the visit prescribed is to some determined church or oratory, not merely to any church. Thus, the Portiuncula Indulgence is granted for visiting a church of the Franciscans.[58] Such visits to determined churches are not included in the provisions of Canon 929. For it reads: "The visit to an undetermined church or undetermined oratory." If the document of indulgence mentions a particular church, even those who are leading a community life may not visit their own chapel instead. Moreover, not every community falls within the terms of the privilege. The Canon enumerates those living in community "in pursuit of perfection, for the purpose of education, or for the sake of health." Consequently persons who live together for merely social reasons, or those confined in prisons, are not sharers in the privilege. Again, the houses in which these persons abide must lack a church or public oratory, in order that the inmates may avail themselves of the benefit of the Canon. Therefore, if such a house were in connection with the parish church or contained a public oratory as defined in Canon 1188,2, and at the same time happened to have a chapel, the inmates could not exercise choice, but must needs visit the church or public oratory. Finally, the words of the Canon "in houses erected with the Ordinary's consent," indicate that the privilege is available only for those hospitals, etc., which have been erected with proper approval, and not on private initiative.

The Code grants a similar though greater privilege to Cardinals and the members of their households: "All Cardinals have the faculty of gaining in their own chapels the indulgences for which is prescribed a visit to some temple or public church of the city or place in which the Cardinals actually are sojourning; this privilege the members of their households also enjoy''[59] The same concession is made to residential and titular Bishops by Canon 349,1.

These concessions in favor of Cardinals and Bishops are more extensive than those contained in Canon 929, extending even to instances where visits to specified churches are prescribed. For, whereas Canon 929 adds the qualifying words ''ecclesiae non determinatae'' and ''indeterminati oratorii,'' Canon 239,1 has simply ''visitatio templi alicujus vel aediculae publicae.'' Where the law fails to introduce the distinction between the determined and the undetermined church, we should not introduce it. Therefore Cardinals and Bishops can gain the indulgences by visiting their private chapels, whether the visit prescribed be to any church in general or to a specified place of worship.

Another modification in the matter of visiting churches is seen in the decree of the Congregation of Indulgences of August 2, 1760. With the approval of Clement XIII, the Congregation permitted those members of confraternities and sodalities whom sickness, imprisonment, or a like cause detained, to omit the prescribed visit.[60] By a decision of February 25, 1877, each confraternity and sodality had to have separate recourse to the Holy See in order to participate in this privilege.[61] Finally, on July 16, 1887, it was conceded that for the future the favor of Clement XIII might be enjoyed by each sodality and confraternity, without having made previous appeal to Rome.[62]

Whenever several indulgences, for each of which a visit to a church is prescribed, may be gained on the same day (as, for instance, the toties quoties indulgence on All Souls' Day), a distinct visit is required to gain each indulgence. One visit, however protracted it may be, does not serve to gain more than one indulgence.[63] Physical entrance and departure are required to constitute these distinct visits. One must repair to a place that is actually outside the church, and thence return to the church. Passing to a point nearer the door, or to another altar or pew, and there repeating the prayers, is not sufficient. One must step outside the door before the next visit may be begun.[63a]

As to the time for making the visit, the Code adopts a departure from the old practice, which prescribed that the time for making the prescribed visits extended "from midnight to midnight."[64] In some particular cases, however, it was expressly stipulated that the time for making the visits began with the first Vespers of the feast (about two o'clock P. M. of the preceding day).[64a] Canon 933 enacts the general rule that the time for visiting the church extends from noon of the preceding day until midnight of the indulgenced day itself. To illustrate: The Portiuncula Indulgence, assigned to the second of August, begins at noon, August first, and continues until midnight, August second. This change adopted by the Code originated in a decree of the Holy Office, January 26, 1911.[65]

To conclude the chapter on particular works, it may be stated that the order in which these exercises are performed is left to the choice of the individual. Whether one shall first confess and then make the visit with prayer for the Pope's intention, or whether one shall reverse this order of exercises, is a matter of individual preference. Thus the Congregation of Indulgences decided on May 29, 1759.[66]

Lastly, one visit to the church may be the occasion of fulfilling all the conditions. This does not contravene

Canon 932, which states that an indulgence cannot be gained "by a work to the performance of which one is bound by precept." For neither the visit to the church, nor the prayers, nor the Confession, nor the Communion are obligatory under pain of sin. Nor is Canon 933 contrary to such practice. That Canon declares that several indulgences cannot be gained by one and the same work. But in the present instance, although the visit is the occasion of all the works, these last are really distinct from the visit, are separate works. Besides, since the visit to the church and the prayer for the Pope's intention are usually combined in the document of concession, since special legislation permits the Communion and the visit to be made simultaneously, and since Confession itself is an act of homage to God, all these acts may very aptly be combined on the occasion of a single visit to the church.

NOTES ON CHAPTER IX.

1 Raccolta, XI, v.
1a Beringer-Steinen, "Die Ablaesse," I, 99.
1b Collectanea S. C. P. F., 1693: "Laudabile quidem est mentaliter orare; orationi tamen mentali aliqua semper adjungatur oratio vocalis."
2 Collectanea S. C. P. F., 1072, ad 3.
3 Decr. Auth. S. C. Indul. et Reliq., 100.
4 Decr. Auth. S. C. Indul. et Reliq., 259, ad 2.
5 Decr. Auth. S. C. Indul. et Reliq., 92.
6 Decr. Auth. S. C. Indul. et Reliq., 273, 92.
7 Decr. Auth. S. C. Indul. et Reliq., 92.
8 Decr. Auth. S. C. Indul. et Reliq., 273.
9 Raccolta, 350.
10 Decr. Auth. S. C. Indul. et Reliq., 393, 287, 368.
11 Acta Apost. Sedis, IX, 539.
12 Vermeersch, "Epitome Juris Canonici," II, 210.
13 Acta Apost. Sedis, XII, 18; Vermeersch, "Epitome Juris Canonici," II, 219.
13a Acta Apost. Sedis, XII, 548; Cf. Linzer Quartalschrift, LXXIV, 158.
14 Acta Apost. Sedis, XII, 18.
15 Decreta Auth. S. C. Indul. et Reliq., 273.
15a Acta Apos. Sedis, XIII, 163; Cf. Beringer-Steinen, "Die Ablaesse," I, 904, note 2.
16 Cf. Linzer Quartalschrift, LXXIV, 157; Beringer-Steinen, "Die Ablaesse," I, 904.
16x Acta Apost. Sedis, XIII, 163.
16a Linzer Quartalschrift, LXXIV, 157.

17 Acta Apost. Sedis, XIII, 163.
18 Vermeersch, "Epitome Juris Canonici," II, 219.
19 Tanquaray, "Synopsis Theologiae Dogmaticae," III, 277.
20 Augustine, "The Pastor," 110, note 13.
21 Augustine, "The Pastor," 110, note 13; Cocchi, "Commentarium in Codicem Juris Canonici," I, 86; Maroto, "Institutiones Juris Canonici," I, 252 D.
21a Acta Apost. Sedis, XIII, 163; Beringer-Steinen, "Die Ablaesse," I, 904, note 2.
21b Acta Apost. Sedis, XIII, 163.
21c Augustine, "The Pastor," 110, note 13.
21d Acta Apost. Sedis, XIII, 163.
22 Canon 934, 2.
23 Vermeersch, "Epitome Juris Canonici," II, 219.
23a Beringer-Steinen, "Die Ablaesse," I, 205.
24 Pruemmer, "Theologia Moralis," 556, 2.
25 Decr. Auth. S. C. Indul. et Reliq., 344.
26 Fanfani, "De Indulgentiis," 48.
27 Vermeersch, "Epitome Juris Canonici," II, 220.
28 Pruemmer, "Theologia Moralis," 556, 2.
29 Noldin, "Summa Theologiae Moralis," III, 322a.
30 Vermeersch, "Epitome Juris Canonici," II, 220.
31 Collectanea S. C. P. F., 922: "Preces requisitae in indulgentiarum concessionibus ad adimplendam Summi Pontificis intentionem sunt ad uniuscujusque fidelis lubitum, nisi peculiariter assignentur."
32 Collectanea S. C. P. F., 1693: "An rejicienda sit opinio docens recitationem devotissimam etiam unius Pater et Ave cum Gloria Patri sufficere ad explendam conditionem orandi pro Summi Pontificis intentione, vel potius admittenda opinionn illorum qui requirunt recitationem quinque Pater et Ave, aut orationes aequivalentes? Resp. Detur Decretum in una Briocensi, sub die 29 Maii, 1841 (V. n. 922)."
33 Decr. Auth. Indul. et Reliq., 214.
34 Vermeersch, "Epitome Juris Canonici," II, 216.
35 Decr. Auth. S. C. Indul. et Reliq., 359.
36 Decr. Auth. S. C. Indul. et Reliq., 231.
37 Decr. Auth. S. C. Indul. et Indul., 253, ad 2; 295, ad 2.
38 Decr. Auth. S. C. Indul. et Reliq., 434.
39 Decr. Auth. S. C. Indul. et Reliq., 214.
40 Decr. Auth. S. C. Indul. et Reliq., 231.
41 Decr. Auth. S. C. Indul. et Reliq., 252.
42 Decr. Auth. S. C. Indul. et Reliq., 295, ad 1.
43 Decr. Auth. S. C. Indul. et Reliq., 426.
44 Decr. Auth. S. C. Indul. et Reliq., 231.
44a Decr. Auth. S. C. Indul. et Reliq., 429.
44b Acta Sanctae Sedis, XXXIX, 62.
45 Noldin, "Summa Theologiae Moralis," III, 319 d.
46 Melata, "Manuale de Indulgentiis," 58.
46a Cf. Decr. Auth. S. C. Indul. et Reliq., 291, ad. 1; 399, ad 1; Canon 933.
47 Fanfani, "De Indulgentiis," 45.
48 Decr. Auth. S. C. Indul. et Reliq., 344.
49 Pruemmer, "Theologia Moralis," 554, 6.
50 Pruemmer, "Theologia Moralis," 556, 4.
51 Benedict XIV, const. "Convocatis," XLVIII.
52 Benedict XIV, const. "Inter Praeteritos," 76; Melata, "Manuale de Indulgentiis," 71.
53 Fanfani, "De Indulgentiis," 45.

54 Vermeersch, "Epitome Juris Canonici," II, 218; St. Alphonsus, "Theologia Moralis," VI, 538; Beringer-Steinen, "Die Ablaesse," I, 116.
55 Vermeersch, "Epitome Juris Canonici," II, 218.
56 Decr. Auth. S. C. Indul. et Reliq., 310; Fanfani, "De Indulgentiis," 46.
57 Acta Apost. Sedis, I, 210.
58 Raccolta, 195.
59 Canon 239, 1, xi.
60 Decr. Auth. S. C. Indul. et Reliq., 222.
61 Decr. Auth. S. C. Indul. et Reliq., 431.
62 Collectanea S. C. P. F., 1680.
63 Decr. Auth. S. C. Indul. et Reliq., 399.
63a Beringer-Steinen, "Die Ablaesse," I, 122.
64 Decr. Auth. S. C. Indul. et Reliq., 434.
64a Decr. Auth. Indul. et Reliq., 291, ad 4; 434, ad 1; Acta Sanstae Sedis, XX, 63; Beringer-Steinen, "Die Ablaesse," I, 128.
65 Acta Apost. Sedis, III, 64.
66 Decr. Auth S. C. Indul. et Reliq., 214.

CHAPTER X.

TRANSFER, SUSPENSION, AND CESSATION OF INDULGENCES.

Indulgences are subject to transfer, suspension, and cessation. A transfer may effect either the time or the place assigned for gaining the indulgence. An indulgence attached to a particular place, such as a church, is transferred when that church is removed and another built in its place within fifty years.[1] Again, the authority in whose competence it is to grant indulgences may require that any indulgence attached to a definite place be transferred to another place.

Transfer as to time is regulated by the Code. As a rule indulgences for which a definite time is fixed are those which are to be gained on the feasts of our Lord and the Saints. By liturgical law, these feasts are transferable. Liturgy distinguishes various elements in feasts, of which only two need be considered here, namely, the Mass and Office of the feast, and the external solemnity. Moreover, the transfer of the feast may be either permanent or occasional, according to the rules of Liturgy. With this premised, one may state that in regard to those feasts which are attended with external solemnity, the indulgence follows the solemnity. That is to say, if the solemnity is transferred to another day (whether the Mass and Office are transferred or not), the indulgence is also transferred. On the other hand, if the solemnity is not transferred (though the Mass and the Office are), neither is the indulgence transferred. Referring to feasts which have only a Mass and Office but no solemnity, the indulgence is transferred if a perpetual transfer of the feast is made. But if the transfer is only occasional, then the indulgence remains fixed to the day on which the feast should have been celebrated.[2] Indulgences granted for novenas and similar exercises, either preceding or following feasts, will be transferred or not, depending on whether or not the feast is transferred as to Mass and Office only, or also as to solemnity. In the case of feasts without solemnity, the transfer of novena indulgences will depend on whether the transfer of the feast is perpetual or only occasional, the novena indulgence being transferred in the former case, not in the latter.[3]

In this connection one point is noteworthy. It is that no one may take advantage of the transfer of a feast in order to gain an indulgence twice. To illustrate: Suppose that an indulgenced feast is celebrated in the universal Church on March the twenty-fifth. For liturgical reasons obtaining in Diocese K, that feast and its accompanying solemnity are transferred to March twenty-eighth. A Catholic may gain the indulgence outside the Diocese K on March the twenty-fifth. Or, if he so desires, he may enter the Diocese K on March the twenty-eighth, and gain the indulgence there. But he is not able to gain it elsewhere on March the twenty-fifth, and gain it again in the Diocese K on March the twenty-eighth.[4]

Suspension of an indulgence occurs when, during a certain interval, it cannot be gained, but, that interval having elapsed, the indulgence can again be gained without the intervention of authority. For instance, the indulgence attached to the Way of the Cross is suspended if the stations are temporarily removed, and it remains suspended until they are replaced.[5] The most familiar example of the suspension of indulgences occurs during the year of Jubilee, when, by express will of the Sovereign Pontiff, most indulgences applicable to the living are suspended.[6]

Cessation of indulgences differs from suspension in that an indulgence, having ceased, does not revive without the intervention of the competent authority. There are many ways in which such cessation may take place. For example, an indulgence ceases by express revocation of the competent authority. Thus, by a decree of the Congregation of Indulgences of August 3, 1899, all indulgences of more than one thousand years were revoked.[7] Moreover, any indulgence in the granting of which the express stipulation was made—by some such phrase as "ad beneplacitum nostrum"—that it should endure only for the life-time of him who granted it, ceases at the death of the granter. But those issued without contrary qualifications are presumed to be perpetual, participating, as they do, in the nature of privileges.[8]

Personal indulgences necessarily cease with the death of the physical person or with the legitimate extinction of the moral person to whom they were granted. It is noteworthy that the unjust suppression of a moral person in no wise effects the forfeiture of that person's rights. Therefore, when such a moral person is restored, indulgences it may have enjoyed before the suppression revive without the necessity of a new concession. In 1815 the Congregation of Oratorians in the city of Turin asked Pope Pius VII for a re-grant of the indulgences they had had before their suppression by the state. The Pontiff replied that they had never lost the indulgences; for, he said: "You were oppressed, not suppressed; the suppression was not at all legal."[9] If the moral person is dormant for one hundred years, it is by that very fact extinct, and the indulgences it may have possessed cease.[10] But as long as at least one physical person survives to represent the moral person, the latter is reputed alive, and the indulgences continue.[11]

Local indulgences cease with the complete and permanent destruction of the place to which they were attached. Thus, an indulgenced church or altar loses its indulgence when completely and permanently razed. By complete destruction is here meant that the place ceases to exist physically, morally, and in the estimation of men. A church, therefore, which had undergone so many alterations at various times as to be physically different from the edifice to which the indulgence was originally attached, would still enjoy the indulgence, because morally and in the estimation of men it remains the same church.[11a] Permanent destruction, when the term is used in connection with a local indulgence, implies that the place, having been razed, is not rebuilt. This seems to be the interpretation which Canon 924,1 puts upon the words of Canon 75. Pending the rebuilding of the destroyed church, the indulgences are simply suspended.[11b] Formerly an indulgenced place, if restored at any time, continued to enjoy its privileges.[12] Now, however, the restoration must be made within fifty years, under the same title, and in the same, or nearly the same location,[13] i. e., within twenty or thirty paces of the old site.[13a] It is worthy of note that the desecration of a place does not induce the loss of indulgences,[14] but a mere suspension of them.[14a]

Real indulgences, those attached to Rosaries, Crucifixes, medals, etc., cease only when the thing ceases to be or is sold. In view of the wide difference of opinion on this point, it seems advisable to quote the pertinent legislation of the Code: "Indulgences attached to chaplets or other things cease only then when the chaplets or other things entirely cease to be or are sold."[15] A Crucifix, for example, will lose its indulgence when the Corpus is broken beyond repair (prorsus desinit esse), not when the Corpus is transferred from one cross to another, or even broken with a fracture that can easily be repaired.[15a] As to Rosaries, Vermeersch correctly observes: "The beads are blessed, and not the chain."[16] Accordingly, the chain may be broken and entirely replaced with new links, the beads may be scattered and arranged in different order, without losing the indulgence. New beads may be substituted for broken ones indefinitely, provided that at no single time such a considerable number of new beads be substituted for the old that in the estimation of men the identity of the Rosary would be changed, for in that case the condition "prorsus desinit esse" would be verified and the indulgence would be lost.[16a]

As to the exchange of indulgenced articles, Canon 924,2 affirms that the only exchange causing the loss of indulgences is exchange by sale. Fanfani quotes the same Canon to prove that indulgences are lost if the articles, once used by the first owner, are donated to another.[17] The conclusion is entirely unwarranted. In explanation of his opinion, Fanfani says: "It is a general rule that real indulgences, applied to various articles, by use become quasi-personal indulgences of those who first use the articles as owners for the purpose of gaining the indulgences."[18] This view is indeed in conformity with the old legislation on the subject,[18a] but not with the new law. For by a declaration of the Sacred Penitentiaary made in 1921, these indulgences are simply real indulgences and there is in them no note of the personal indulgence.[19] Hence it matters not whether those articles be given away before or after being used, the indulgence still adheres to them. Moreover, the owner may give or lend his chaplet or other indulgenced article to another, and the latter while using it gains for himself all the indulgences. The original owner on receiving back the article likewise can gain all the indulgences for himself. For it is only by the sale or complete destruction of the article that the indulgences are lost.[19a] As to loss through sale, Vermeersch succinctly states a point of very practical interest: "To avoid every semblance of usury, it has frequently been declared that indulgences are lost through a sale subsequent to the blessing of the article (cf. resp. 16 Julii, 1887). But there is nothing to prevent the merchant's having chaplets which he has already sold blessed; and that, even though the price has not yet been paid."[20] It frequently happens that on the occasion of a mission priests sell articles of piety, which are indulgenced. The faithful select the article, ask the priest to bless it, after the blessing receive it from his hand, and then tender the price of the article. Canon 924,2 is not in opposition to this practice. For in this case, as Vermeersch observes, the bargain of sale is really made before the blessing of the article takes place.[21] The same cannot be said of the following case: A priest on the mission receives from a firm a number of Rosaries. On the day they are received he blesses them all and lays them away. Then, from time to time, as people have need, he sells them one by one. (However, selling the entire supply to one individual at one time would not alter the solution). Here it is evident that those Rosaries lose the indulgence, according to the prescription of Canon 924,2.

The reference in the preceding paragraph to the sale of indulgenced articles suggests a few remarks on the Church's legislation to prevent abuses in the matter of indulgences. That the Church had to suffer much from some of her subjects' malpractice in connection with indulgences is a historical fact too patent to require emphasis here.[22] It is to her credit that the Church promptly counteracted incipient abuses with laws calculated to suppress misuse of indulgences.[23]

It has been noted above that one of the first forms of general indulgences in the Church was the indulgence for alms.[24] It soon became customary for ecclesiastical authorities to entrust the publication of these indulgences, as well as the collection of alms connected therewith, to itinerant preachers, called questors.[25] But the same "accursed lust for gold" that had corrupted one of the twelve and had misled Simon Magus, also beguiled these questors, inducing them to abuse the charge they had received. In order to restrain that cupidity, the Fourth Lateran Council condemned the questors' excesses, and prescribed the form they were to observe in future in eliciting the generosity of the faithful in behalf of pious causes.[26] In 1311 the Council of Vienne deprecated the practice of those questors "who, for a sum of money, remit the third or fourth part of imposed penance, who release from Purgatory (as they falsely claim) three or four souls of parents or friends of those who give them money." The Council enacted that all these should be condignly punished by their Bishops, no regard being paid to the privileges and immunities they might claim as questors.[27] The Council of Trent finally abolished the name and office of questors, decreeing that in future the Ordinary, with the aid of two members of his chapter, should attend to the publication in his diocese of indulgences and similar spiritual favors, and to the collection of alms offered in view of these favors.[28] The same Synod demanded that the Bishops, assembled in provincial synods, should ferret out whatever abuses were practiced in the matter of indulgences and report them to the Holy See, in order that proper steps might be taken for their suppression.[29]

In order to realize the reformatory measures taken by the Tridentine Council, Pius IV in 1562 prescribed that henceforth all concessions of indulgences must be given gratis.[30] To secure the same end, Pius V, in 1567 revoked all indulgences for the gaining of which alms-giving was prescribed.[31] In 1571 the same Pope deprived of the fruits of their benefices and placed under interdict all Bishops and prelates of higher rank who used indulgences and similar spiritual favors as a means of gain. Other persons incurred excommunication reserved to the Holy See for practicing such simony.[32]. The Constitution "Apostolicae Sedis," issued by Pius IX in 1869, renewed the excommunication with which Pius V punished those who trafficked in indulgences, but the penalties against higher ecclesiastics were not renewed.[33]

Canon 2327 of the Code contains the penalties now in force against traffickers in indulgences: "Those who make gain of indulgences are ipso facto punished by excommunication simply reserved to the Holy See." Unlike the Constitution of Pius V, the present Canon punishes the abuse of indulgences alone, and does not extend to other spiritual favors.[34] According to the common law, this excommunication does not effect Cardinals, though Bishops are subject to it.[35] "Quaestum facientes" of Canon 2327 are those who actually accept money for granting indulgences, either by ordinary or delegated power, or for promulgating indulgences that have been granted. The act of selling indulgenced articles is punishable by this excommunication only when the usual price of the indulgenced article is increased in view of its being enriched with indulgences.[36]

NOTES ON CHAPTER X.

1 Canon 924, 1.
2 Canon 922.
3 Canon 924.
4 Decr. Auth. S. C. Indul. et Reliq., 435, ad 5.
5 Fanfani, "De Indulgentiis," 53.
6 Benedict XIV, const. "Cum Nuper ad Nos," XVIII, 1.

7 Collectanea S. C. P. F., 2063.
8 Fanfani, "De Indulgentiis," 54.
9 Decr. Auth. S. C. Indul. et Reliq., 285.
10 Canon 102, 1.
11 Canon 102, 2.
11a Beringer-Steinen, "Die Ablaesse," I, 176.
11b Beringer-Steinen, "Die Ablaesse," I, 176.
12 Vermeersch, "Epitome Juris Canonici," II, 208, 2 c.
13 Canon 924, 1.
13a Acta Sanctae Sedis, XIX, 94.
14 Decr. Auth. S. C. Indul. et Reliq., 396.
14a Beringer-Steinen, "Die Ablaesse," I, 176.
15 Canon 924, 2.
15a Fanfani, "De Indulgentiis," 54.
16 Vermeersch, "Epitome Juris Canonici," II, 208, 3.
16a Beringer-Steinen, "Die Ablaesse," I, 842.
17 Fanfani, "De Indulgentiis," 55.
18 Fanfani, "De Indulgentiis," 55.
18a Decr. Auth. S. C. Indul. et Reliq., 34; 78; 447; cf. Beringer-Steinen, "Die Ablaesse," I, 843. The latter corrects his view, conforming his opinion to the new legislation. See Beringer-Steinen, "Die Ablaesse," I, Appendix, pg. 585.
19 Acta Apost. Sedis, XIII, 64.
19a Canon 924, 2.
20 Vermeersch, "Epitome Juris Canonici," II, 208, 3.
21 Vermeersch, 'Epitome Juris Canonici," II, 208, 3.
22 Chelodi, "Jus Poenale," 67, 4.
23 Chelodi, "Jus Poenale," 67, note 6.
24 Cf. above, 30.
25 Ayrinhac, "Penal Legislation in the New Code of Canon Law," 236.
26 Harduin, "Acta Conciliorum," VII, 66.
27 C. 2, de Poenitentiis et remissionibus, V, 9, in Clementinis.
28 Conc. Trident., sess. XXI de Reformatione, c. 9.
29 Conc. Trident., sess. XXV de Reformatione, Decretum de Indulgentiis.
30 Const., "Decet Romanum Pontificem," Magnum Bullar., Rom. II, 100.
31 Const., "Etsi Dominici Gregis," Magnum Bullar., Rom. II, 228.
32 Const., "Quam Plenum," Magnum Bullar., Rom. II, 323.
33 Const., "Apostolicae Sedis," II, 11.
34 Ayrinhac, "Penal Legislation in the New Code of Canon Law," 238.
35 Canon 2227, 2.
36 Caviglioli, "Censurae Latae Sententiae," 119; Chelodi, "Jus Poenale," 67, 4; Ayrinhac, "Penal Legislation in the New Code of Canon Law," 238; Fanfani, "De Indulgentiis," 26; Vermeersch, "Epitome Juris Canonici," III, 527.

BIBLIOGRAPHY

I. Sources and Periodicals

Acta Apostolicae Sedis, Rome, 1909-1924.
Acta Sanctae Sedis, Rome, 1865-1908.
American Ecclesiastical Review, Philadelphia.
Analecta Ecclesiastica, Rome, 1892-1911.
BENEDICTI *XIV, Bullarium,* Prati, 1846.
Canones et Decreta Concilii Tridenti, Taurini, 1913.
CAVALLERA: *Thesaurus Doctrinae Catholicae,* Paris, 1920.
Codex Juris Canonici, Rome, 1917.
Collectanea S. C. de Propaganda Fide, Rome, 1907.
Corpus Juris Canonici, Leipzig, 1922.
Decreta Authentica S. C. Indulgentiarum et Reliquarum, Ratisbon, 1884.
DENZINGER-BANNWART: *Enchiridion Symbolorum et Definitionum,* Freiburg, 1922.
Dublin Review, Dublin.
Der Katholik, Mainz.
KIRCH, C.: *Enchiridion Fontium Hist. Eccles. Antiquae,* Freiburg, 1914.
Magnum Bullarium Romanum, Luxenburg, 1727.
MANSI, J. D.: *Sacorum Conciliorum Nova et Amplissima Collectio,* Venice, 1759.
The Month, London.
Periodica de Re Canonica et Morali, Bruges.
Theologische-Praktische Quartalschrift, Linz.
Zeitschrift fuer Katholische Theologie (Z. K. T.), Innsbruck.
The Raccolta, Philadelphia, 1881.

Authors

ALPHONSUS, ST.: *Theologia Moralis,* Rome, 1900.
AMORT, *Historia Indulgentiarum,* Venice, 1738.
AUGUSTINE, C.: *A Commentary on Canon Law,* St. Louis, 1921.

Augustine, C.; *The Pastor*, St. Louis, 1923.
Ayrinhac: *Penal Legislation in the New Code of Canon Law*, New York, 1920.
Bastien: *Tractatus de Jubilaeo Anni Sancti*, Brussels, 1901.
Baumgarten: *Henry Charles Lea's Historical Writings*, New York, 1909.
Bellarmine, Card. Robert: *De Indulgentiis et Jubilaeo Libri Duo*, Cologne, 1599.
Benedict XIV: *De Synodo Dioecesana*, Parma, 1764.
Beringer-Hilgers: *Die Ablaesse, ihr Wesen und Gebrauch*, Paderborn, 1895.
Beringer-Steinen: *Die Ablaesse, ihr Wesen und Gebrauch*, Paderborn, 1922.
Bouvier-Oakley: *On Indulgences*, London, 1848.
Catholic Encyclopedia, New York, 1917.
Caviglioli: *Censurae Latae Sententiae*, Turin, 1919.
Chelodi: *Jus Poenale*, Trent, 1920.
Cocchi: *Commentarium in Codicem Juris Canonici*, Turin, 1922.
D'Ales: *Dictionaire Apologetique de la Foi Catholique*, Paris, 1915.
D'Ales: *La Theologie de Tertullien*, Paris, 1905.
Eckius, Joannes: *Enchiridion Locorum Communium Contra Lutherum*, ———, 1533.
Fanfani: *De Indulgentiis*, Rome, 1919.
Ferraris: *Prompta Bibliotheca*, Rome, 1899.
Genicot: *Institutiones Theologiae Moralis*, Brussels, 1922.
Grisar: *Luther*, Freiburg, 1911.
Herder: *Kirchenlexicon*, Freiburg, 1882.
Hilgers: *Die Katholische Lehre von den Ablaessen und deren Geschichtlichen Entwicklung*, Paderborn, 1914.
Layman: *Theologia Moralis*, Moguntiae, 1723.
Lea: *History of Auricular Confession and Indulgences*, Philadelphia, 1896.
Lehmkuhl: *Theologia Moralis*, Freiburg, 1914.
Lepicier: *Indulgences, their Origin, Nature, and Development*, London, 1895.
Maroto: *Institutiones Juris Canonici*, Rome, 1921.

MAUREL: *Le Chretien Eclaire sur la Nature et L'Usage des Indulgences*, Paris, 1865.
MELATA: *Manuale de Indulgentiis*, Rome, 1892.
MORINUS: *Commentarius Historicus de Disciplina Poenitentiae*, Paris, 1651.
MIGNE: *Patrologiae Graecae Cursus Completus* (MPG), Paris, 1886.
MIGNE: *Patrologiae Latinae Cursus Completus*, (MPL) Paris, 1850.
NOLDIN: *Summa Theologiae Moralis*, New York, 1920.
OTTEN: *A Manual of the History of Dogmas*, St. Louis, 1917.
PALMIERI: *Tractatus de Poenitentia*, Rome, 1879.
PASTOR: *History of the Popes*, St. Louis, 1898.
PAULUS: *Geschichte des Ablasses in Mittelalter*, Paderborn, 1922.
PESCH: *Institutiones Theologiae Dogmaticae*, Freiburg, 1920.
PRUEMMER: *Theologia Moralis*, Freiburg, 1923.
PUTZER: *Commentarium in Facutates Apostolicas*, New York, 1893.
RAUSCHEN: *Eucharist and Penance*, St. Louis, 1913.
SABETTI-BARRETT: *Compendium Theologiae Moralis*, New York, 1919.
SUAREZ: *Opera Omnia*, Paris, 1856.
TANQUARAY: *Synopsis Theologiae Dogmaticae*, New York, 1920.
THOMAS, ST.: *Summa Theologica*, Rome, 1894.
VERMEERSCH: *De Formulis Facultatum S. C. de Prop. Fide Commentarium*, Bruges, 1922.
VERMEERSCH: *Epitome Juris Canonici*, Mechlin, 1921.
VERMEERSCH: *Theologia Moralis*, Mechlin-Rome, 1923.

DEUS LUX MEA

THESES

QUAS

AD DOCTORATUS GRADUM

IN

Iure Canonico

APUD UNIVERSITATEM
CATHOLICAM AMERICAE

CONSEQUENDUM

PUBLICE PROPUGNABIT

FRANCISCUS EDUARDUS HAGEDORN

SACERDOS DIOECESIS KANSANOPOLITANAE

IURIS CANONICI LICENTIATUS

HORA IX A. M., DIE XXVII MAII, A. D. MCMXXIV

Universitas Catholica Americæ

Washingtonii, D. C.

Facultas Juris Canonici

1923-1924

No. 22

I. De Promulgatione Legum Ecclesiasticarum. Canones 8-11.

II. De Legis Canonicae Subjecto. Canones 12-14.

III. De Interpretatione Legum Ecclesiasticarum. Canones 17-19.

IV. De Executione Rescriptorum. Canones 52-59.

V. De Personis. Canones 87-89.

VI. De Domicilio et Quasi-Domicilio. Canones 90-95.

VII. De Consanguinitate et Affinitate. Canones 97-98.

VIII. De Divisione Dioecesis. Canones 215-217.

IX. De Romano Pontifice. Canones 218-221.

X. De Synodo Dioecesana. Canones 356-352.

XI. De Consultoribus Dioecesanis. Canones 423-428.

XII. De Religiosis. Canones 487-491.

XIII. De Confessoribus Religiosarum. Canones 518-530.

XIV. De Novitiorum Institutione. Canones 553-558.

XV. De Ritibus et Ceremoniis Baptismi. Canones 755-761.

XVI. De Tempore et Loco Missae Celebrandae. Canones 820-823.

XVII. De Ministro Sacrae Communionis. Canones 845-852.

XVIII. De Loco ad Confessiones Excipiendas. Canones 908-910.

XIX. De Translatione et Cessatione Indulgentiarum. Canones 922-924.

XX. De Subjecto Indulgentiarum. Canones 925-930.

XXI. De Impedimentis in Genere. Canones 1035-1042.

XXII. De Quibusdam Dispensationibus Matrimonialibus. Canones 1043-1046.

XXIII. De Impedimento Mixtae Religionis. Canones 1060-1064.

XXIV. De Forma Celebrationis Matrimonii. Canones 1094-1103.

XXV. De Violatione Ecclesiae. Canones 1171-1175.

XXVI. De Sepultura Ecclesiastica. Canones 1239-1242.

XXVII. De Abstinentia et Jejunio. Canones 1250-1254.

XXVIII. De Ratione Studiorum in Seminariis. Canones 1364-1366.

XXIX. De Judiciorum Ecclesiasticorum Notione, Objecto, et Divisione Ratione Objecti. Canones 1552-1553.

XXX. De Foro Competenti. Canones 1556-1558.

XXXI. De Notario, Promotore Justitiae, Vinculi Defensore. Canones 1585-1590.

XXXII. De Loco et Tempore Judicii. Canones 1636-1639.

XXXIII. De Restitutione in Integrum. Canones 1687-1689.

XXXIV. De Extinctione Actionum. Canones 1701-1705.

XXXV. De Confessione Partium. Canones 1750-1753.

XXXVI. De Iis Qui Testes Esse Possunt. Canones 1756-1758.

XXXVII. De Appellationibus in Causis Matrimonialibus. Canones 1986-1989.

XXXVIII. De Conatu Delicti. Canones 2212-2213.

XXXIX. De Notione Excommunicationis. Canones 2257-2259.

XL. De Poenis in Violantes Sigillum Sacramentale. Canones 2269, 889-890.

XLI. Errores circa Formam Regiminis Ecclesiae.

XLII. De Cessatione Potestatis Pontificiae.

XLIII. De Concordatis.

XLIV. De Relatione Ecclesiae ad Principium Libertatis Religiosae.

XLV. De Jure Gladii.

XLVI. De Potestate Episcopali.

XLVII. An Potestas Jurisdictionis Episcopalis sit Immediate a Deo.
XLVIII. De Ratione Parochiatus.
XLIX. De Potestate Civili Quoad Matrimonia.
L. De Unione inter Ecclesiam et Statum.
LI. Sources of International Law.
LII. Extradition.
LIII. General Rights and Obligations of States.
LIV. Recognition of a State.
LV. Jurisdiction over Vessels.
LVI. Immunities and Privileges of Diplomatic Agents.
LVII. The Monroe Doctrine.
LVIII. Consular Agents.
LIX. Protectorates, Suzerainties, Spheres of Influence, Mandates.
LX. Piracy.

Vidit Sacra Facultas:

PHILLIPPUS BERNARDINI, J.U.D., S.T.D., Decanus.

HUBERTUS LUDOVICUS MOTRY, J.C.D., S.T.D., a Secretis.

Vidit Rector Universitatis:

✠ THOMAS J. SHAHAN, S.T.D., J.U.L.

LIFE.

Francis Edward Hagedorn was born at Pierce City, Missouri, April 29, 1897. He received his primary education in the parochial schools of that city, his secondary education at Conception College, Conception, Missouri. On September 29, 1916, he entered St. Meinrad Seminary, St. Meinrad, Indiana, and was ordained to the priesthood May 15, 1921. He entered the Catholic University of America, Washington, D. C., October 2, 1922, and attended the lectures of Monsignor Filippo Bernardini, in Canon Law, of Rev. Dr. John A. Ryan, in Moral Theology, of Monsignor Edward A. Pace, in Educational Religion, of Rev. Dr. Hubert Motry and Rev. Dr. Valentine Schaaf, both in the School of Canon Law.

To his professors and instructors he extends his grateful appreciation for their services in his behalf.

www.ingramcontent.com/pod-product-compliance
Lightning Source LLC
LaVergne TN
LVHW050220080826
844660LV00012B/442

* 9 7 8 0 8 1 3 2 2 2 1 3 4 *